"Living in [...] and sin, is difficult [...] us that the mess we live in is, like us, awaiting a future redemption. Read along as Dan teaches us to navigate these challenges and anticipate the arrival of our perfect hope, Jesus, who will make an end of death and make his blessings flow as far as the curse is found."

RUSSELL MOORE, *President, Ethics and Religious Liberty Commission of the Southern Baptist Convention*

"This is exactly the book our culture needs right now. In this age when we're saturated with reminders that we live in a fallen world every time we turn on the news, *Life in the Wild* gives Christians a much-needed dose of perspective—and hope." **JENNIFER FULWILER,** *SiriusXM radio host; and author of One Beautiful Dream*

"Beautifully written, and with great insight into both the ideas of history and the contemporary mind. Dan DeWitt provides an exciting retelling of the glory, the desperation, and the hope of humankind. Many will gain wisdom for living 'life in the wild' of this present world as they enjoy this work. Those who make the journey through its pages will learn that there is another Message that offers far more happiness than all the offerings of the messages of the secular age. This is a work of great joy."

ERIC C. REDMOND, *Assistant Professor of Bible, Moody Bible Institute*

"Dan DeWitt is one of this generation's most articulate and compelling writers. His keen insight brings clarity to some of life's most difficult questions. Everyone should read this book."

THOMAS WHITE, *President of Cedarville University, Cedarville, Ohio*

"An intriguing view into the story of us! Dan gifts readers with a biblical survival guide for the wilderness of life." **V.ROSE,** *singer and songwriter*

"This is a fresh and urgent field guide to life in the real world—the world of brokenness, tragedy, and disappointment. Dan DeWitt gives us not only clarity and realism, but also wonderful hope, as he consistently and carefully points us to Christ. It did me good to read it!"

SAM ALLBERRY, *speaker, Ravi Zacharias International Ministries; editor, The Gospel Coalition; author of Is God Anti-Gay?*

"*Life in the Wild* is the book I have been waiting for from Dan DeWitt. At the turn of every page, the aroma of Christ is sweet. This work will make you laugh, weep, and shout for joy."

KEVIN JONES, *Associate Dean at Boyce College; co-author of Removing the Stain of Racism from the Southern Baptist Convention*

"Life is wild, and by 'wild' I don't mean awesome and fun. Life can be wildly tough. In *Life in the Wild*, Dan DeWitt teaches us why life is terrible at times and where to turn. But there's hope and you'll find our Hope shared in these pages!" **TRILLIA NEWBELL,** *author of God's Very Good Idea*

"We all recognize that something is wrong in us and around us. *Life in the Wild* helps us embrace the truth that even when we feel small, the gospel is 'big enough to make sense of sinkholes and shark bites.' "

CARMEN LABERGE, *author of Speak the Truth: How to Bring God Back into Every Conversation; and host of The Reconnect*

"Dan does a wonderful job of unpacking the Genesis story of humanity and how the gospel of Jesus is what we need to survive and make sense of the wild world we live in. As a church-planting pastor, I will be eager to get this book into the hands of new believers, young Christians, and discipling groups!"

LUCAS PARKS, *Lead Pastor of Village Church Belfast and Acts 29 Country Director for Ireland*

"*Life in the Wild* is a manifesto of hope in the midst of a hopeless world. When so much darkness surrounds us, Dan DeWitt extends a beautiful and biblical lifeline of light in the gospel. I wish every young Christian, seeker, or skeptic would pick up this book to find the hope we're all looking for."

JAQUELLE CROWE, *author of This Changes Everything: How the Gospel Transforms the Teen Years; and editor of The Rebelution*

"This world is full of unspeakable tragedy. The gospel contains unparalleled hope. Convinced of both realities, Dan DeWitt guides us through Genesis 3 with wit, warmth and wisdom. Let *Life In The Wild* show you afresh the depths of our fallenness and the heights of God's redeeming love. It will do your soul much good." **GLEN SCRIVENER,** *evangelist; and author of 321*

DAN DEWITT

LIFE
IN THE
WILD

FIGHTING FOR FAITH IN
A FALLEN WORLD

thegoodbook
COMPANY

*To Nannette, my mom,
a model example of what it looks like to
fight for faith in a fallen world.*

Life in the Wild
© Dan DeWitt/The Good Book Company 2018

Published by:
The Good Book Company
Tel (US): 866 244 2165
Tel (UK): 0333 123 0880
Email (US): info@thegoodbook.com
Email (UK): info@thegoodbook.co.uk

Websites:
North America: www.thegoodbook.com
UK: www.thegoodbook.co.uk
Australia: www.thegoodbook.com.au
New Zealand: www.thegoodbook.co.nz

ISBN: 9781784981693 | Printed in the UK

Design by André Parker

CONTENTS

FOREWORD

BY MIKE COSPER

FOUNDER AND DIRECTOR, HARBOR MEDIA

If you walk in the door of many—if not most—Western churches on a Sunday morning, you'll be greeted with smiles, with hot coffee, and with the thunderous and victorious sounds of contemporary worship music. You'll sing choruses about how great God is and how great our love for God is, and hear a sermon about how great life with God is or how wonderful it is that we're changing the world for the better.

And then you'll go home. There, you'll find miserable news on television. You'll find pill bottles lining kitchen and bathroom cabinets that are supposed to remedy everything from sinus problems to schizophrenia. You'll find pictures of relatives who suffered brutally with any manner of disease, or photos of loved ones who died in traffic accidents, were killed by roadside bombs in Iraq or Afghanistan, or simply left one day, content to live their lives without any connection to home or family.

In other words, you'll return to the real world, where bad news greets us all too often and where the triumphal sounds of Sunday morning ring hollow. There's no doubt that the Scriptures offer joy and peace, but they also offer suffering at the hands of lions and swords and crosses and thorns.

As Dan DeWitt puts it—and as so many others have put it—"life sucks." And as much as we'd like to paper over that thought with platitudes and happy praise choruses, the paper is thin, the suffering is real, and all too often our worlds come crumbling down around us.

In *Life in the Wild*, Dan invites us to face these realities and to see their origins in the book of Genesis. He traces the textures of brokenness and exile across the map of history, finding resonance in art and literature, from *Les Misérables* to *Star Wars* to the works of C.S. Lewis and Francis Schaeffer. It's an unflinching look at the reality of life in a fallen world, and life in a world that all too often sucks.

There's an old joke about a certain kind of Christian who, upon falling down the stairs, says, "Well, I'm glad that's over with." This reflects a spirit of inevitability regarding suffering, but also a sense of indifference on the part of the God who is sovereign over all of creation. It's a kind of baptized stoicism—a belief that because suffering is inevitable, we had all better suck it up and deal with it as it comes. Thankfully, you will find none of that misery here.

Instead, Dan invites us to face the reality of life in the wild— life in the exiled aftermath of Genesis 3—in order to see the pathways that might guide us through it. Rather than embrace the kind of doped-up optimism for which Christianity has long been critiqued (thank you, Karl Marx), or its opposite (the fatalistic assumption that misery is inevitable), Dan invites a sober look at the world as it is in order to better understand the redemptive promises of the gospel. As an old Puritan prayer puts it, we see the light of the stars much more brightly from the valleys. We live in a valley, but the hope of the gospel is a bright light.

And here's the thing: if we want to participate meaningfully and redemptively in a fallen world, there is no other starting place than to acknowledge the truths about life in exile. By acknowledging that life sucks, we can begin to look for hopeful pathways through its thorns and thistles, and we can begin engaging our friends and family and neighbors from a place of honesty.

Life in the Wild is an exploration of those pathways. Whether talking about God's truthfulness and trustworthiness, the challenges we face from ecological disaster, or the challenges we face in a world that's eroding the meaning of marriage and gender, Dan addresses each with a sense of grace, love, and compassion.

His approach refuses the pressures of compromise on one end and the temptation to be combative, bombastic, and pharisaical at the other. It is a refreshing vision of life in a fallen world.

Above all else, this book is *pastoral*. Rather than dealing with these topics in the abstract, or burying them in the coded language of theology and philosophy textbooks, *Life in the Wild* is an immensely readable book. Each chapter moves from ideas to concrete practices—invitations to transform our thinking and doing—that make life in a dark world more bearable, more hopeful, and more open to the possibilities of joy that remain in its midst.

I believe you'll find that *Life in the Wild* is as joyful as it is sober and as winsome as it is confrontational. Most of all, I

INTRODUCTION
THE HUMAN TRAGEDY

It was a warm spring afternoon two weeks before my high-school graduation. My Italian mother came to my room carrying two small bowls with silver spoons planted in scoops of vanilla ice cream. We sat on my bed to talk.

Just an aside: if an Italian woman brings you food when it's not mealtime there's usually a catch.

I looked suspiciously at my mom as I enjoyed the unexpected treat. My mom's never been one to beat around the bush. "Your father and I are going to separate," she told me. I wasn't entirely surprised.

Two weeks later, on a Friday evening, I walked across a platform in my school gymnasium to receive my diploma. That next morning my dad backed his pickup truck out of our gravel driveway on West Chambers Street in Jacksonville, Illinois. Life would never be the same.

That's not to say that life wasn't good. It just wasn't the same. And how could it be? My two siblings and I were all out

11

of school. I was the last to graduate and I was heading off for college. And now my parents were getting divorced. Nothing could remain the same.

My mom had a simple way of putting everything into perspective. "Life sucks," she would say. "What are you going to do about it?" That pretty well summed up her philosophy of life. Things go wrong. Bad things happen to good people. Good things happen to bad people.

What are you going to do about it?

My mom is a tough-minded, godly lady with an unquestionable work ethic and a bent toward the artistic side. That's my way of saying she's pretty amazing. And her approach to life has rubbed off on me.

Living in the Land of Meh

Mom's confident expectation that things wouldn't always, or even usually, go as planned, along with her resolve to make the best of it, seemed biblical to me. After years of studying theology, I find it still seems right. Anyone who has read the first few chapters of Genesis knows that something has gone terribly wrong. To quote Shakespeare, "Something is rotten in the state of Denmark."

Life sucks. What are you going to do about it?

As Dorothy learned in *The Wizard of Oz*, we're not in Kansas anymore. We are far from the Garden of Eden, described at the beginning of the Bible. Our ancient parents were expelled from that perfect place. We've been exiles on an eastward journey away from paradise ever since the human rebellion in Genesis 3. The good life is a fading image on the rearview mirror of our hearts.

So, what are you going to do about it?

Are you going to try to go back? It's not there anymore, you know. All of that was done away with in the biblical flood. And speaking of the flood, it only took our race six chapters of the Bible to get from creation to cosmic judgment. We're not very good at making the most of things.

In fact, an earthly utopia only lasted for two chapters in the biblical story. Yup, we could only get through fifty-six verses before making a mess of things. Well, technically speaking, Adam and Eve botched it. But if we were in their place, we probably wouldn't have made it out of the first couple of chapters either. If I were the first man, I probably wouldn't have gotten beyond Genesis chapter one before blowing it.

We no longer reside in Eden. Now we live in the land of Meh, a world seemingly ruled by Murphy's Law. If it can go wrong it often does. And things have gone terribly wrong.

Even if you don't believe in God, you may have an intuitive sense that things are off kilter. But does that even make sense? If there is no God, if there is no grand design, then why does it feel as though something good has gone bad?

On the other hand, if you do believe in God, does that offer any practical help for dealing with all the mess life throws at you?

What does the Bible say about our human dilemma? Can it explain the world we live in that is marked by both design and disorder, by both beauty and horror? It's my belief that the first three chapters of Genesis shed light on the world we live in. Understanding these early chapters of this ancient manuscript can allow us to better understand the daily news headlines.

Disagree? Open a Bible and take a look yourself. Perhaps my book can serve as something of a tour guide.

A Promise Made in a Garden

As you start out in Genesis, you will see that there was a time, long ago, when our forefathers knew pure, unadulterated, undiluted, untarnished goodness. Can you imagine that? But that was a long time ago, before the devil (described in Genesis as a serpent) enticed the first people to reject God's perfect plan for their lives and make their own choices about good and evil.

This is how they lost paradise:

"You will not certainly die," the serpent said to the woman. "For God knows that when you eat from [the tree of the knowledge of good and evil] your eyes will be opened, and you will be like God, knowing good and evil."

When the woman saw that the fruit of the tree was good for food and pleasing to the eye, and also desirable for gaining wisdom, she took some and ate it. She also gave some to her husband, who was with her, and he ate it.

Then the eyes of both of them were opened, and they realized they were naked; so they sewed fig leaves together and made coverings for themselves.

Then the man and his wife heard the sound of the LORD God as he was walking in the garden in the cool of the day, and they hid from the LORD God among the trees of the garden. But the LORD God called to the man, "Where are you?"

He answered, "I heard you in the garden, and I was afraid because I was naked; so I hid."

And he said, "Who told you that you were naked?
Have you eaten from the tree that I commanded you
not to eat from?"

The man said, "The woman you put here with me—she
gave me some fruit from the tree, and I ate it."

Then the LORD God said to the woman, "What is this
you have done?"

The woman said, "The serpent deceived me, and I ate."
(Genesis 3 v 4-13)

And so, in just a few verses, the first people went from a perfect relationship with God to hiding from him; they went from obeying God's words to listening to the devil instead; and now they would have to leave the safety and beauty of the garden and find a way to exist in the wild.

In this book we'll think about what was lost in the Garden of Eden as described in Genesis. We'll look at the consequences of the curse of sin, the results of grasping for the fruit of moral self-rule, and the effects of human rebellion that indelibly mark our lives.

But I hope to do something more. I hope to paint a brutally honest picture of what living in a fallen world looks like. And I want to paint it in red hues that depict a bloody battle waged over the souls of men.

God promised to undo what was done, to restore what was lost, and to bring us back into his presence, where we can again experience his goodness. That's the point of the promise the Creator made to the first couple in Genesis 3.

> *So the LORD God said to the serpent, "Because you have*
> *done this … I will put enmity between you and the*
> *woman, and between your offspring and hers;* ***he will***
> ***crush your head, and you will strike his heel."***
> *(Genesis 3 v 14-15, bold text mine)*

Adam and Eve had to leave the garden. Instead of flourishing in a garden of beauty and perfection, they had to live "in the wild"—in a world stained by sin. But these rebels were given a promise strong enough to sustain them over the years to come. A promise that someone from their family line, one of Eve's offspring, would defeat the serpent once and for all.

Life in the wild wouldn't be easy. But like my mom says, "Life sucks." What could they do about it?

The truth is, *only God could do something about it*. That's why the rest of the Bible, from Genesis 3 forward, is about God coming to do what Adam should have done in the first place. God would come in the flesh, step into human history, and write himself into this twisted story to begin setting things right.

Jesus came to obey God's word; protect his bride, the church; and defeat the serpent. That's what Adam should have done. That's what Jesus came to do. That's the story of the Bible.

This single promise offered in the garden serves as a beacon of light to guide our steps in the fallen terrain. It offers hope and help for people like you and me. We are messed-up people living in a messed-up place. If we just look inside the pages of Genesis, we will discover a description of our situation.

Maybe we will even find rest for our road-weary souls.

Is Life a Tragedy or Comedy?

In literature the terms tragedy and comedy have specific meanings. A tragedy is a story in which someone falls from a favored position. A comedy is generally a story in which someone ascends from a humble station. In simple terms, a tragedy has a happy beginning and a sad ending. A comedy is the opposite.

Think of the biblical story as both tragedy and comedy. It begins and ends in joy. But it is mostly filled in between with a dark struggle to restore what was lost so early on, so long ago.

The opening and closing acts are about goodness. We live between acts now where we can see light by looking far back, perhaps further than our eyes will allow, or by gazing out into the indefinite future. It can seem nearly impossible at times to find our way in the here-and-now, in what I will describe throughout out the book as *the wild*.

This fallen world, the wild, hasn't changed much since Adam and Eve's time. The headlines have basically been the same since Genesis 3. But one day the page will turn, the king will return, and history will be set aright. One day goodness will be restored.

In the Garden of Eden, humanity lived in God's presence. And throughout the Bible we see hints that one day the garden will be restored. There will again be a place where we can live in peace with our Creator.

That's why both the tabernacle and the temple, the buildings where the Israelites worshipped God, had ornate organic designs. These were symbols of nature that pointed *back* to what was lost in Eden and *forward* to a day when Eden will be restored.

The Blessed In-Between

Followers of Jesus live in what theologians describe as the "already but not yet," a time of struggle undergirded by living hope. Christ has come; that's what the Gospel stories are about, but his kingdom is not yet fully realized on earth. Eden has yet to be restored. It won't be until his final return that things are ultimately put right.

We see Jesus, we believe in Jesus, and we wait for Jesus. Yet still we suffer. But the authentic gospel, the pure message of Jesus offered in the Bible, offers real and rugged answers for life's dark places. That's what we'll discover in this book.

Many within the church misrepresent the challenge of living in a fallen world by glossing over the reality of human pain. Some Christians deny suffering by acting as though it is somehow optional—as if faithful Christians need not concern themselves with such things. Prosperity-peddling preachers make it sound as though heaven is attainable on earth if we can just muster up enough faith—or send them enough money.

There's only one problem with offering Eden now. The *fake it until you make it, don't worry, be happy, smile your problems away, enjoy your best life now* sort of Christian clatter offered through a lot of Christian broadcasting and bookstores rings hollow when real hardships come—and they do. They always do, to all of us.

The Bible leads us to expect this. It is a book of suffering. The first book to be written in the Old Testament actually wasn't Genesis. It was Job, a story about a man who lost everything. Nearly half of the Psalms are considered to be songs of lament or songs of suffering. The final book of the Bible, Revelation, is a letter to churches that are being persecuted.

But the Bible is also a book of hope. Our suffering leads us somewhere, to someone. The gospel message says that we are not in Eden—we are in the wild. But we are on a journey out of the wild, and a new Eden lies ahead.

Reality about the wild—and hope in the wild—is what we're all after.

So yes, life sucks. That's what Genesis 3 tells us to expect. But if we trust in Jesus, he will help us to live well in the wild, as we wait for the day when he returns and calls us out of the wild and into the perfection to come.

CHAPTER 1

INTO THE WILD

*"So the LORD God banished him from the Garden of
Eden to work the ground from which he had been
taken. After he drove the man out, he placed on
the east side of the Garden of Eden cherubim and a
flaming sword flashing back and forth to guard the
way to the tree of life."*

GENESIS 3 V 23-24

Can you imagine what Adam must have felt the day after he and Eve were kicked out of the garden? Perhaps he prayed over and over again that it was all just a dream, and that he would wake up in Eden.

If it was a dream, it was surely a nightmare. But it was a true nightmare. Images of a rushed exit, an angel, a flaming sword, footsteps in the garden that made his heart tremble, accusations hurled from husband to wife, from wife to serpent, were all burned into his brain in a way that time itself would never erase.

The poet John Milton captured this scene in the title of his famous poem: *Paradise Lost*. Adam lost paradise. He lost everything. And not just for himself, but for his beautiful bride, his future children, his grandchildren, and for you and for me.

Outside the garden would have been undeveloped—*wild*. Before the rebellion, God had commanded Adam to extend the garden outward, to "fill the earth and subdue it" (Genesis 1 v 28). Now, instead of being on the inside spreading the garden out, he and his bride stood on the outside, where wildness prevailed, with no way of getting back in.

Instead of living in the center and extending God's rule, they were exiles living on the margins. Adam and Eve were now outsiders. They would have to find a way to survive—and maybe, just maybe, even to flourish, outside of paradise.

But is that even thinkable? *Life sucks*. What could Adam do about it?

The Stories We Discover Ourselves In

It's easier to read a story than live one. I was reminded of this recently when watching a documentary about the terrorist plane attacks of 9/11.

College students at the school where I teach were only toddlers when the worst terrorist attack in US history took place. It could be easy for them to watch programs about it with a sort of detached curiosity. Not me. I vividly remember where I was the moment I learned of the attacks.

I was driving my old Volvo station wagon up River Road in Louisville, Kentucky, heading to seminary chapel after an early morning fishing trip.

On this particular day I noticed the lack of airplane traffic over the city. With a busy commercial airport and the UPS international hub downtown, I was used to seeing planes coming and going. But not that day.

I was listening to the radio when a reporter interrupted the program and with a tense voice announced that a plane had flown into the World Trade Center.

The rest of the day was surreal. Chapel was canceled. We were all encouraged to spend time with our families and pray.

To my surprise, the documentary made me relive the nausea and disbelief of that day. I felt sick to my stomach.

Those who weren't born then, or weren't old enough to understand, likely watch reports of 9/11 with more objectivity than subjectivity. They see the events as something that happened to others, but they don't feel themselves in the story.

I fear the same is true for many of us with the story of God and the great human rebellion—what theologians call "the fall." We can read it from a distance without ever having to consider how it affects us. But the reality is that it *does* affect us, more than we care to realize.

This isn't just Adam and Eve's story. It's your story—and my story—too.

Every bad thing we experience flows from the fact that our ancestors rebelled against God. And we discover ourselves in this great rebellion, all taking up various roles in this dark play from the very moment of our births. Scripture says we were born in sin (Romans 5 v 12). We were born in Adam's rebellion.

How Being Disconnected from God Affects Us

We are separated from our Creator. This is the source of all forms of death: physical and spiritual. Like a lamp when just unplugged, our light may flicker momentarily but it will refuse to shine. We are disconnected from the source of all energy, the Creator of life.

But what exactly does it mean to be disconnected from God? The New Testament authors use a short word to describe this condition: *death*. That's a powerful word. Five letters that, when put together, take on the form of our greatest enemy. We are physically dying and spiritually dead from the day we are born.

We might look fine on the outside, but on the inside something is wrong. We know it. And one day our bodies will catch up with the sad state of our souls.

We all know this is true. Experience exposes our inner decay. We don't do the things we know we should do. We do the things we know we shouldn't do. We have a really hard time living consistently with the purposes we pursue. It's in these moments that we feel the sting of death on the inside.

Let me ask you a personal question if that's okay. *How long have you been working on you?* You might respond with a smirk, "My whole life!" You know that's right. Now, let me ask you another question: *How's that working out for you?*

You see, you probably know deep down that you can't fix you. The Bible says the problem is even deeper than that. No one else can fix you either. Humanly speaking that is. You are disconnected from the Maker of all things—and he is the only one who can make you right again.

But it's not a quick one-time fix. And to be brutally honest, it will kill you. But the "you" that will die in this process is not the person you were meant to be. It's the rebel who resists God's ways to your own harm.

You will discover that, in the death of the old you, something lovely will emerge. Not perfect, in any earthly sense, but something that's in the process of being restored and one day will be fully returned to its original purpose.

At times it may even feel as if the cure is worse than the disease. But it will only feel this way temporarily. The apostle Paul, writing in the New Testament, says this:

> *I consider that our present sufferings are not worth*
> *comparing with the glory that will be revealed in us.*
> *(Romans 8 v 18)*

Paul is saying that the glory we will experience when Christ returns will far outweigh any suffering we face now.

You may want to dismiss this as merely spiritual sentimentality, just religious rhetoric. But here's what's harder to dismiss. You've tried pretty hard to help yourself. And it really hasn't worked yet. You have a sinking suspicion that it never will.

That's because when Adam and Eve rebelled against God, they broke off the most important relationship, not just for themselves, but also for the entire human race. The Bible scholar James P. Boyce describes three implications of this separation from God: (1) we are alienated from God, (2) we've lost God's favor, and (3) we've lost our acceptance with him. Let's consider these a little more closely.

1. Spiritual Aliens on a Silent Planet

Because of the rebellion, we are alienated from God. We're foreign to him and he's foreign to us. We don't belong to him. He doesn't belong to us.

The term *alienated* simply means that something becomes foreign or unfamiliar to something else. The two things no longer have a natural connection. They are separated.

Separation can be a good thing. If you've ever been to a zoo, you know that while you might enjoy standing next to the lion pit, you're thankful for the barriers keeping the giant cat from making you lunch. You're glad you're alienated from the lion.

But separation from God is far from good for us.

I sometimes hear secular humanists argue that we don't need God for humans to be happy and flourish. Humanism is basically a way of life where God is left out of the equation. Some think a religion-free society will be a better place. But history shows us that leaving God out of society doesn't lead to flourishing—it actually leads to horror.

Most humanists today, however, really advocate more of a soft secular society where faith in God simply fades into the background over time.

But can this kind of "nice atheism" offer humans a foundation for meaning? Is John Lennon right in his song "Imagine"? Is life really better if there is no heaven or hell, no God? Consider what the famed British atheist Richard Dawkins has admitted in his popular quote about a world without God:

> *In a universe of … blind physical forces and genetic replication, some people are going to get hurt, other people are going to get lucky, and you won't find any rhyme or reason in it, nor any justice. The universe that we observe has precisely the properties we should expect if there is, at bottom, no design, no purpose, no evil, no good, nothing but pitiless indifference …*

DNA neither knows nor cares. DNA just is. And we dance to its music.

The sort of atheism that Dawkins promotes is really not what most secularists would have in mind. He's too angry to be a viable candidate to speak on behalf of most humanists. But regardless of how we feel about his personal tone, I think he's absolutely right. In a world without divine purposes, we are left with no categories of evil or good. We're left in a sea of pitiless indifference, where God and his goodness are alien to us.

2. Loss of Favor

The significance of this second point can be easily missed. If we are separated from God, then how does losing his favor change anything? Consider this passage from the Bible from Paul's letter to the Colossians:

The Son is the image of the invisible God, the firstborn over all creation. For in him all things were created: things in heaven and on earth, visible and invisible, whether thrones or powers or rulers or authorities; all things have been created through him and for him. He is before all things, and in him all things hold together.
(Colossians 1 v 15-17)

What happens if we kick Jesus out of our culture? For starters, we can't kick him out. He's the Creator. He's not going anywhere. But what would happen if a society tried as hard as they could to make him irrelevant to all of life, to push him as far to the fringes as possible?

I think we would find ourselves in the kind of world described by Richard Dawkins, where good, evil, design, and purpose all slip through our fingers like sand. It would be a world filled with lots of things, all of which mean nothing.

But nobody lives like that. Not even atheists like Richard Dawkins. I have a large, beautiful coffee-table book titled *A Better Life: 100 Atheists Speak Out on Joy and Meaning in a World Without God*. There's even a spread devoted to Richard Dawkins, about how he finds meaning in life.

Interesting, isn't it? I thought he said that at bottom there is no meaning. Maybe Dawkins doesn't really *believe* that after all. He certainly doesn't live that way.

That's because every fiber of our being cries out that beyond the stars in the night sky, there is more than pitiless indifference. And deep down we know we are disconnected from this source of meaning. Maybe that's because all of our efforts to find our way back to the garden, to a place of real purpose, have ended in failure.

King David, in the nineteenth psalm, says the heavens "declare the glory of God." But, in seemingly sharp contrast, the apostle Paul says in the first chapter of his letter to the Romans that the heavens reveal "the wrath of God." We live in this tension between glory and wrath, where we must fight to keep faith in the goodness of God in the midst of a fallen world. But why does it always seem to be just out of our reach, no matter how hard we try?

3. Despicable Me (and You)

It gets worse. Not only are we aliens to God, and not only have we lost his favor: *we are his enemies*. That means there are no merely passive unbelievers. There are only active rebels: enemies.

We are co-conspirators with the serpent:

Now the serpent was more crafty than any of the wild
animals the LORD God had made. He said to the
woman, "Did God really say, 'You must not eat from
any tree in the garden'?"

The woman said to the serpent, "We may eat fruit from
the trees in the garden, but God did say, 'You must
not eat fruit from the tree that is in the middle of the
garden, and you must not touch it, or you will die.'"

"You will not certainly die," the serpent said to the woman.
"For God knows that when you eat from it your eyes will be
opened, and you will be like God, knowing good and evil."

When the woman saw that the fruit of the tree was good
for food and pleasing to the eye, and also desirable for
gaining wisdom, she took some and ate it. She also gave
some to her husband, who was with her, and he ate it.
(Genesis 3 v 1-6)

Like Eve, we doubt God's trustworthiness. We prefer to do things our way and not his. We have committed divine treason. Like a person who is considered by the government to be an enemy of the state, we are a people without a country. We are a people on the run.

The Bible describes us as "children of wrath" (Ephesians 2 v 3, ESV). We are rebels from our very first breath, every one of us. And the only thing God has to give us, apart from Jesus, is wrath. That's why the Bible says that "people are destined to die once, and after that to face judgment" (Hebrews 9 v 27). One day every human will stand before the Creator and give an accounting for their rebellion.

Our only hope is divine amnesty. Amnesty is what happens when a government offers complete immunity for crimes committed against the state. Because our rebellion is ultimately against the Creator, we need amnesty from heaven.

A lot of people try to earn this sort of immunity. They might go to church or mass and hope that religious activity makes them closer to God. But that's kind of like climbing a ladder and bragging about being closer to the sun. The distance is far too great for our humble efforts to be meaningful.

We can't close the gap. Nothing we can do on our own will ever get us back to him again. The chasm is too great. He has to stoop down and come to us.

And he did.

Finding Faith in a Fallen World

God so loved the world that he gave his only Son (John 3 v 16). Jesus came on a mission to seek and save sinners (Luke 19 v 10). He offered his life as a sacrifice for rebels like us (Romans 5 v 6). The apostle Paul describes how Jesus turns rebels—who are dead on the inside, who deserve God's wrath—and makes them alive again:

> *But because of his great love for us, God, who is rich in*
> *mercy, made us alive with Christ even when we were*
> *dead in transgressions—it is by grace you have been*
> *saved. (Ephesians 2 v 4-5)*

The death we experience in life is undone by God's Son. The effects of our rebellion are all reversed in Christ. In Jesus we are no longer alienated from God. We regain his favor, and we are no longer enemies.

Elsewhere Paul describes this as a legal transaction:

[Jesus] was delivered over to death for our sins and was raised to life for our justification. (Romans 4 v 25)

He died in our place to pay the debt owed to God because of our rebellion. And when God raised Jesus from the dead, it was a sign to the entire world that Jesus' payment was sufficient. God's wrath for human rebellion was completely realized.

It's impossible to fully grasp the depth of God's forgiveness. We tend to think of sin the same way we think about junk food. So we focus on our most recent splurge, or perhaps the biggest and best unhealthy snack we've ever experienced. We rarely think about it in a cumulative way, considering, for example, all of the bad food decisions we've made in a given day, week, month or year, or in an entire lifetime.

I remember one day, while traveling, it hit me how much junk food I had eaten on my short trip. I had lived off of donuts, pizza, cookies, French fries, and greasy cheeseburgers. It didn't bother me much until that very moment.

At most, I thought about it one bite at a time. But as I awaited our departure on the runway, I had a more sober assessment. I considered the total effect of my choices. Maybe it was because my stomach was experiencing turbulence and we hadn't even taken off yet.

Imagine all of the junk food you've ever eaten piled up before you: congealed processed cheese and gritty sugary gravy running down a mountain of meaty pancakes and pepperoni pizza. The smell alone would force you into strict, New-Year's-resolution-like dietary changes.

Once you get over your nausea from reading the previous paragraph, consider the following: we sometimes think about sin in this same kind of moment-by-moment way. So we think Jesus' death is really about our most recent sin or about the biggest sin in our past.

But Jesus died for *all* of our sins. We have to consider our rebellion in total. His death was for every single act of disobedience and selfishness we commit in the entirety of our lives; and not just ours, but for those of the entire world.

That's why Paul can say that God is both just and the justifier (Romans 3 v 26). Justice is not watered down so that we can come back to God. Jesus completely obeyed God, without a hint of rebellion, and then gave his life for ours. Jesus satisfied God's just standard. And Jesus freely offers his grace to insurgents like us.

We are like window-shoppers standing on the sidewalk and gazing at something in a store display that we could never afford on our own. Imagine that a generous individual in the store notices our fixed gaze and longing expression, purchases the item for us, and walks out of the store and freely hands it to us.

This is something like the position we are in longing for things to be made right here on earth. We certainly can't fix things on our own. We've demonstrated that. Someone has to purchase that and give it to us as a gift.

This is similar to how the Bible explains God's forgiveness. Jesus paid for our rebellion so we can have peace with God. We didn't earn it. We can't earn it. It's a gift. It has to be a gift or we could never get it. Someone else had to purchase it for us. The Bible calls this *grace*.

Join the Family

Once we experience Jesus' grace, the New Testament describes our relationship with God through Christ in powerful family terms. The author of Hebrews writes:

> *Both the one who makes people holy and those who are made holy are of the same family. So Jesus is not ashamed to call them brothers and sisters.*
> *(Hebrews 2 v 11)*

This means that in addition to not being God's enemies, we are actually now his children—the brothers and sisters of Jesus himself.

But none of this happens automatically. In our natural rebellion we will resist this offer of divine amnesty. We might prefer to do self-improvement projects instead of submitting to God's design. We might think the issue isn't that bad or that it might get better on its own. But really we know that it won't. Nothing has worked yet.

If you've never had a life-transforming encounter with Jesus, I encourage you to consider that through him you can have peace with God. By trusting Jesus, by placing your faith in his sacrifice and resurrection, you can connect to God's purpose for your life and experience forgiveness.

You will learn that as you follow Jesus, you will need to constantly come back to him as the source of meaning and purpose—what the Bible describes as remaining in him (John 15 v 4).

And if we have already put our trust in Christ, there is so much to be thankful for, however hard life may be right now. Instead of being disconnected from God and his blessings, we have a restored relationship with him (Colossians 1 v 21-22). We experience his favor and find acceptance through Christ. Even when we continue to sin—and we will—it has been paid for in full by God the Son.

Does this mean we can avoid living in the wild? No. The consequences of Genesis 3 will continue until the day Christ returns. But we can live well in the wild, and we can have confidence and hope, because we know that Jesus is leading us through it, and will keep us safe in him until we reach the other side.

> *God has said,*
> *"Never will I leave you;*
> *   never will I forsake you."*
> *So we say with confidence,*
> *"The Lord is my helper; I will not be afraid.*
> *   What can mere mortals do to me?" (Hebrews 13 v 5-6)*

Your mission, should you choose to accept it, is to fight, in the midst of our fallen world, to keep faith in God's good promise first made in the Garden of Eden—a promise, through Christ, to end our alienation and restore us to a right relationship with him; a promise to end evil and restore goodness. And in a fallen world, it may very well be that only a promise of this magnitude is strong enough to keep you.

CHAPTER 2

WHERE ARE YOU?

"Then the man and his wife heard the sound of the LORD God as he was walking in the garden in the cool of the day, and they hid from the LORD God among the trees in the garden. But the LORD God called to the man, 'Where are you?'"

GENESIS 3 V 8-9

In Charles Dickens' classic *A Christmas Carol*, there is a powerful exchange between the Ghost of Christmas Present and Ebenezer Scrooge. Scrooge notices something moving near the foot of the spirit's robe. When he asks about it, the ghost reveals two malnourished and miserable children grasping his ankles.

"Beware them both," the spirit says, "but most of all beware this boy, for on his brow I see that written which is Doom, unless the writing be erased." When Scrooge asks if the children have no one to help, the ghost retorts with Scrooge's own words: "Are there no prisons? Are there no workhouses?"

The children are symbols of the effect of Scrooge's selfishness. Their names are *Ignorance* and *Want*, and they glare at him with condemning eyes. Scrooge knows their accusations are well-placed.

These children directly reflect the result of Scrooge's meanness. But what if they showed something different—the offspring of humanity itself? Then I think they could be renamed *Guilt* and *Shame*.

"Spirit. Are they yours?" Scrooge asks. "They are Man's," the spirit replies. So it is with guilt and shame. They are the children of humanity. They cling tightly to our side. They will not easily be shooed away.

They are nearly as old as time itself. They were born in the garden when Adam and Eve first rebelled. They are the offspring of forbidden desires.

Guilt and Shame: Their Origin Story

Guilt and Shame were foreign to the garden before the rebellion. But as Eve wiped the juice of the forbidden fruit from her lips, these emotions fell over her like a dark shadow. Their silhouettes followed her until her dying day. She would be buried in their cold presence.

Adam followed in Eve's footsteps, and two more shadows were born. Guilt and Shame are conceived in rebellion. They resemble their parents. They have their father's eyes and their mother's smile. We cannot deny that they are ours.

To live in the wild, outside of Eden, is to be intimately acquainted with them. We know them well, far better than we wish. We would love to part with them. But they won't leave us alone. Here's their origin story:

> *When the woman saw that the fruit of the tree was*
> *good for food and pleasing to the eye, and also desirable*
> *for gaining wisdom, she took some and ate it. She also*
> *gave some to her husband, who was with her, and he*
> *ate it. Then the eyes of both of them were opened, and*
> *they realized they were naked; so they sewed fig leaves*
> *together and made coverings for themselves.*
> *(Genesis 3 v 6-7)*

Adam and Eve knew they weren't wearing clothes before they disobeyed God. They weren't stupid. But now their nudity became something they felt the need to cover up. And a few verses later it made them hide from the very Lord who had created them:

> *The LORD God called to the man, "Where are you?"*
>
> *He answered, "I heard you in the garden, and I was*
> *afraid because I was naked; so I hid." (Genesis 3 v 9-10)*

Adam and Eve went from enjoying the presence of their Creator to hiding behind the trees he had made. For the first time, they knew the debilitating power of guilt and shame.

Separating Siblings

Though Guilt and Shame are twins, born only seconds apart, they are not identical. I've heard it said that guilt is what we experience when we get away with doing wrong; shame is what we experience when we get caught. There is some truth in this, though shame goes a lot deeper than just getting caught.

Guilt is usually tied to an event: *I did something bad.* Shame is tied to a person: *I am bad.* Guilt is the wound. Shame is the scar. Guilt is isolated in the individual. Shame is contagious.

When you violate God's laws, how do you feel? If you're a believer, hopefully you feel guilt (though we are sadly very good at burying guilt and ignoring our disobedience). When we do feel guilt, it is quickly joined by shame. Guilt says, "You did something wrong." Shame says, "That's why you need to hide. You're no good. You deserve to live in darkness. Come with me; I'll lead the way."

To liken Guilt and Shame to the children in Dickens' *A Christmas Carol*, Guilt is the girl and Shame is the boy. And as the ghost says, "Beware of them both, but most of all beware the boy, for on his brow I see that written which is Doom." What Guilt begins, Shame expands. Doom is written on his forehead.

No one can share in your guilt, but many can share in your shame. The child whose father is imprisoned, the wife whose husband is unfaithful, the daughter with an abusive mother— they all share in the shame. They feel as though their self-worth is lessened. Shame wraps its arms around their ankles tightly—allowing them to walk, but never to run.

In this way shame is far less logical than guilt. Guilt is connected to events that can be defined in objective journalistic categories: who, what, where, when, and why. But shame is far less concerned with details.

If we are going to survive, and even thrive, in the wild, we will need to learn to deal with both our guilt and our shame. We need solutions for addressing the facts of wrongdoing— our guilt. But we also need help navigating the emotional trauma we experience in the wake of our sins. Both of these children will threaten our existence. But beware the boy.

Fighting for Faith

Let's begin with guilt. When we do something wrong, when we disobey, when we sin, we need to own up to our actions. We can't just run and hide like Adam and Eve.

Because I have four kids I have a lot of examples of this. Here's one. My wife walked into our kitchen to discover a trail of ants outlining drops of honey across the tile floor. She followed the ants and honey into the dining room where they led under our dinner table. Crouching down she discovered our son Josiah, then four years of age, with a guilty look on his face and an empty honey jar.

But we don't have to look to children. Even adults want to run when we've done something wrong. I guess it's human nature in the wild. That's what Adam and Eve did when they heard the Creator approaching:

> *Then the man and his wife heard the sound of the LORD God as he was walking in the garden in the cool of the day, and they hid from the LORD God among the trees of the garden. (Genesis 3 v 8)*

Did they really think they could hide from God forever? Do we? But still we try. Why? The first thing we need to do is to come out of the darkness and into the light.

Wonderfully, Jesus promises to accept us as we repent of our sin and turn to him for forgiveness. In fact, he once told a story about a rebellious son to illustrate the power of God's forgiveness. The son rejected his father and set out to spend his inheritance on parties and pleasure (Luke 15). But when times got tough, he turned his heart toward home, and began the long trip back.

He rehearsed his speech over and over. With every passing step his heart beat faster. He had treated his father so badly. He had basically told his dad he wished he were dead. So he planned to beg for mercy and ask to be treated as a mere servant.

But as he turned the final stretch and saw his home on the horizon, a strange thing happened. He could make out the figure of a grown man running toward him in the distance. I wonder if he thought it was someone sent to keep him from coming onto the property. That's exactly what he deserved.

At some point he probably stopped and squinted to make sure his eyes weren't fooling him. It was his father. And the expression on his dad's face was not of anger but of unbridled joy.

Why would Jesus give us such a sweet picture of God's love? Wouldn't it have been better to show a stern and angry father so we would know we can't mess around with God? There are other places in Scripture where God is shown as angry. Why not here?

To understand why, let's dig further.

The Better Brother

In his story, Jesus includes an older brother who never left the father's house. He was the "good" brother. But he refused to celebrate his brother's return. He rejected his father's invitation to join the party for his little brother's homecoming.

Jesus included the older brother to show the religious leaders how he felt about their lack of empathy and compassion for "outsiders" (Luke 15 v 2). This is in many ways the main point of the parable: Jesus *loves* sinners.

He came to seek and save the lost (Luke 19 v 10). That's good news for rebels like us. Before telling this story of the prodigal son, Jesus told two other stories of lost things—about a sheep and a coin. In both there is a thorough search for the lost item. But in the story of the prodigal son there is no search—only a grumpy older brother.

But in that culture, it was the older brother who should have gone to find his wayward younger brother.

Let's not miss this. Jesus tells three stories. In the first two, lost things are carefully searched for—but not in the third. There is no search for the younger brother. The older brother is like the religious leaders who don't want their lost brothers to come back.

That's the point: *Jesus is a better big brother.* In the face of these defiant religious leaders who think they are too good for the outsiders, Jesus shows that he has come to do what the big brother should have done. He has come to find us— the lowly, prodigals, rebels, delinquents, sinners. Us. He came to find us.

Jesus shows us that God is eager to forgive. Like the father, he is waiting to see us turn the bend on our return home. The walk home won't be easy. But this is the only way to deal with our guilt. We have to agree with God that what we have done is wrong and seek his forgiveness. We have to come home.

We will see him, you know. We will see him waiting for us, waiting to forgive us. That's why he sent his firstborn Son to find us. He wants us to come back.

Shame, however, won't let go as easily as guilt. Even after God our Father forgives our guilt, we will still suffer under our shame. Long after our guilt is paid for, shame can maintain a strong grip on our hearts. It is relentless. It has Doom written on its brow.

That's because shame's approach is to deal with the *person* rather than the act of wrongdoing. Wrestling with shame requires a different strategy than that for guilt. Shame will tell you that you are irredeemable, that the father won't accept you. "You've gone too far this time. You can never come home," Shame tells us.

Outside In

I don't want to oversimplify this. Shame is messy. But let me give you a place to start. We have to begin by reminding our souls that we are forgiven and our worth is found in Christ. As one preacher said, "We have to quit listening to ourselves and start talking to ourselves."

Psalm 103 gives a great model for us to follow. In this psalm, King David spends nineteen verses talking to himself. He addresses his audience in the opening verse: "Praise the LORD, *my soul*." David begins talking to himself in verse one and doesn't mention anyone else until the final few lines.

You should take some time soon, maybe even now, to read Psalm 103 for yourself. Go ahead and do it. Trust me, it will be good for your soul. I'll be waiting here for you when you finish.

Pause...

Okay, done? Good deal.

In verse 1 David calls upon all his "inmost being" to praise God. It's as though he believes he is able to rule over his emotions and call them to a proper perspective of God. This is a very Jewish/Christian understanding of what it means to be human.

If you've seen the animated movie *Inside Out*, then you're familiar with the opposite view. Although the movie seems to be about a young girl named Riley, we quickly learn that it isn't really about her. It's all about her emotions.

The first emotion we meet is *Joy*. She's a fairy-like character with a bright smile and optimistic outlook. She stands at the control panel of Riley's life. We then meet what seems to be her opposite, *Sadness*—a short girl with glasses who sounds a bit like Eeyore from *Winnie the Pooh*.

Fear is a tall skinny guy whose main task is to keep Riley alive. "We made it through the day without dying. I consider that an unqualified success!" he says at one point.

Disgust is a trendy-looking girl dressed in green. Her goal is to keep Riley from socially awkward situations and from eating broccoli. Last but not least, we meet *Anger*, whose job is making sure Riley is never treated unfairly.

These emotions pull the strings in Riley's life. In fact, if we take this perspective to a logical conclusion, there is no Riley. There are only chemical reactions in her brain—emotions—that determine her actions. The idea that she is a person who supervises her life is only an illusion.

This is far from the biblical view of what it means to be human. David *commands* his soul to praise God, and his inmost being to bless the Lord. This is the path toward removing our shame. We have to quit listening to the voice of shame in our heads and start preaching to our souls. We can't let our emotions run the show.

Praise the LORD, My Soul

David specifically commands his soul to bless God for the following benefits: he forgives all our sins, heals all our diseases, crowns us with love and compassion, renews our strength, and satisfies our soul (Psalm 103 v 3-5). That's quite a benefit package!

If you feel as if you're losing in the struggle with shame, I'd encourage you to read Psalm 103 everyday and internalize it. Command your soul to praise God. Review the many benefits that David outlines. Claim them as your own. When you come to a benefit in the psalm such as forgiveness, you could say or write, "I am forgiven."

I also encourage you to make sure you're in a supportive church community. Shame grows in isolation. You need Christian friends, particularly in the context of your church, who can rehearse these truths with you. You need help in preaching to your soul.

God can use your guilt and shame to prompt you to turn to him. We don't need to stagger under their burden; we can bring them to the cross.

By accepting Jesus' sacrifice for our sins, we can be declared not guilty. In this sense we don't have to fear facing God one day. Our rebellion is covered. That's wonderful news!

This is what God did for Adam and Eve. Before they left the garden, God killed an animal to provide clothing to cover their nakedness. He covered their shame. That's what he does. It's his speciality. And this act of sacrifice pointed forward to another sacrifice that would forever cover over the shame of our rebellion.

But I should warn you: outside the garden, even though we live in the wild as believers, there aren't easy solutions for dealing with guilt and shame.

Because we are fallen people, living in fallen bodies, in a fallen world, we will continue to rebel at various times in various ways. We have stubborn hearts. God has given us his Spirit to help us fight the battle (Galatians 5 v 16-26), but it is a real conflict that we will be engaged in until our final breath. No one gets a pass.

As you can see, we will have to have fight for faith in this fallen world. Living in the wild is dangerous. But we don't have to be slaves to Guilt and Shame. There is One who conquered them both, and he offers us help and hope. Every time we fall, we can return to him:

> *If we claim to be without sin, we deceive ourselves and the truth is not in us. If we confess our sins, he is faithful and just and will forgive us our sins and purify us from all unrighteousness. If we claim we have not sinned, we make him out to be a liar and his word is not in us.*

> *My dear children, I write this to you so that you will not sin. But if anybody does sin, we have an advocate with the Father—Jesus Christ, the Righteous One. He is the atoning sacrifice for our sins, and not only for ours but also for the sins of the whole world. (1 John 1 v 8 – 2 v 2)*

CHAPTER 3

DAZED AND CONFUSED

*"Now the serpent was more crafty than any of the wild
animals the LORD God had made. He said to the
woman, 'Did God really say…?'"*

GENESIS 3 V I

"**D**id God really say?" This simple question lurks behind
every temptation ever faced by breathing beings. We
may not have had a slithering snake whisper it in our ears,
but we hear this reptilian lie all the time. Too often we fall
for the bait.

I once heard a preacher say, "You can listen and learn—or
you can live and learn." In other words, you can choose to do
right before experiencing the consequence of doing wrong—or
you can choose to do wrong and learn from the consequences.
My goodness, those words ring true. Adam and Eve had to live
and learn. Sadly, bitterly, too often, so do we.

But we face a different problem than Adam and Eve. Our
temptation is not in the serene landscape of a perfect garden.
No, our temptations come to us in the darkness of the wild,

where we have been conditioned to see what is good as evil and where we rebrand evil as good.

Which Ralph Is Right?

The complexities of our situation can be illustrated in the literary battle for a character named Ralph. Ralph first showed up in 1858 in the book *The Coral Island* by R.M. Ballantyne. This successful novel inspired two better-known books, *Treasure Island* and *Peter Pan*. But almost a century later a different author gave Ralph a massive makeover.

In *The Coral Island* Ralph and two friends are stranded on an island in the South Pacific. The three teenagers learn about leadership, see firsthand the influence of the spread of Christianity, and finally make it back home with valuable lessons learned.

In 1954, ninety-six years later, the author William Golding flipped this story on its head with his novel *Lord of the Flies*. Golding admitted that his book was a direct response to *The Coral Island*, even keeping the name Ralph. In Golding's story, Ralph and several other young teen boys are stranded on an island but the theme is gravely different. Instead of learning lessons from the evil they observe in the outside world, they quickly demonstrate that evil is inside each of them.

The boys struggle to find order, end up fighting for power, and devolve into a murderous, monstrous mob. After the gang kills his best friend, Ralph is forced to run for his life through the island, which has been set ablaze. The story ends when a passing naval warship spots the fire and sends out a party to investigate.

The boys instantly resume their childhood natures and begin weeping uncontrollably when the adults discover them. Their innocence is lost. Life will never be the same.

Which Ralph is right? Which author presents a more accurate picture of reality? If we're given our own island, will we avoid evil, learn lessons, and retain a sense of order? Or, will we end up killing the weak and burning the whole place down?

The Battle for You

We live with this strain between innately knowing goodness and yet living in a world corrupted by human rebellion. We can't escape evil. We carry it with us. It's in our blood. We are at war with God, with others, and with ourselves.

That's because deep within our hearts there is an appetite for forbidden fruit. We become indifferent to God and others in our fatal attractions. Our rebellion dulls us to what is truly good. The Bible describes this as suppressing the truth by our wickedness (Romans 1 v 18).

God offers us something far better, but to find it we have to follow his voice. Yet, in the wild, there is always the reverberating echo, "Did God really say?"

Here's what God said: he spoke goodness. God's favorite adjective may well be "good." He uses it a lot. We see it throughout the first two chapters of Genesis. It was God who first called the fruit trees he had created good:

> *Now the LORD God had planted a garden in the east,*
> *in Eden; and there he put the man he had formed.*
> *The LORD God made all kinds of trees grow out of the*
> *ground—**trees that were pleasing to the eye and***
> ***good for food**. In the middle of the garden were the tree*
> *of life and the tree of the knowledge of good and evil.*
> *(Genesis 2 v 8-9, bold text mine)*

God crowns the days of creation with the word *good*. He made everything beautiful. The fruit of the trees he created was both pleasing to the eyes and good for food.

This theme of goodness runs throughout Scripture. In Psalm 34, David tells us to taste and see that God is *good* (Psalm 34 v 8). Jesus calls faithful servants *good* (Matthew 25 v 21). Paul says God will work all things together for the *good* of those who love God (Romans 8 v 28).

But in the wild our vision of the good can be easily blurred. When God's moral standards are moved to our peripheral vision, not only do they become blurry to us, but we drift away from them.

In the wild we will have to learn to refocus our eyes, to reprogram our appetites. If you've ever tried to lose weight, you know how difficult this can be. When you are exercising and dieting, it can seem as though junk food is calling your name in the middle of the night.

"Dan," the bag of chips beckons, "come and eat me. You deserve me. I will make everything better." Yeah, that's why I generally carry around an extra twenty pounds. But some excess weight is nothing compared to the compound effects of cultivating a moral appetite for that which isn't good.

Satan's Whispers

Satan has a way of taking what is good and twisting it into a shape custom-made for our appetites. "For God knows that when you eat from it your eyes will be opened," Satan told Eve, "and you will be like God, knowing good and evil" (Genesis 3 v 5). That's how Satan tripped up Eve. He made evil look good.

He knows how to speak our love language, doesn't he? You can see the shift in Eve's thinking:

> *When the woman saw that the fruit of the tree was good*
> *for food and pleasing to the eye, and also desirable for*
> *gaining wisdom, she took some and ate it. She also gave*
> *some to her husband, who was with her, and he ate it.*
> *(Genesis 3 v 6)*

As we saw earlier, the Bible makes it clear that God made the fruit good for food and pleasing to the eye (Genesis 2 v 9). Its beauty and function were part of his original design. But through Satan's influence, Eve added a new category: the fruit was *desirable for gaining wisdom.*

Did God tell her that? No, he did not. But Eve wasn't focusing on what God said. His words had become blurry to her.

Before the fall, it was God who determined what was good and what was not good. Eve's reach for the fruit was an act of defiance, a decision to draw moral lines where she wished. She was determining for herself what was good and what was not good.

We sometimes do the same. When we look at God's good commands through our peripheral vision, they start to look like something else. They begin to look like prohibitions that hold us back. They look like obstacles instead of guideposts. So we pick up the moral pencil to sketch out our own boundaries.

That's what the boys did in *Lord of the Flies.* The moral boundaries they set reflected the evil in their hearts. Jesus makes it clear that our hearts, too, have darkness within (Mark 7 v 20-23).

Regaining Vision

Since God's moral laws appear distorted when we push them to the margin of our lives, and because we gravitate toward what we focus on, we must develop a renewed vision. To find a guide for living in the wild, we have to fix our eyes on the One who was able to keep all of God's good commands. We must "follow in his steps" (1 Peter 2 v 21).

In my estimation, no chapter in the New Testament illustrates the messiness of living for God in the wild more than Hebrews 11. This passage is often described as the "hall of faith." Before we walk through the famous hall, let's see where it leads:

> *Therefore, since we are surrounded by such a great cloud*
> *of witnesses, let us throw off everything that hinders*
> *and the sin that so easily entangles. And let us run*
> *with perseverance the race marked out for us, fixing*
> *our eyes on Jesus, the pioneer and perfecter of faith. For*
> *the joy set before him he endured the cross, scorning its*
> *shame, and sat down at the right hand of the throne of*
> *God. Consider him who endured such opposition from*
> *sinners, so that you will not grow weary and lose heart.*
> *(Hebrews 12 v 1-3)*

Hebrews 11 commends several biblical characters for their faith in God. They are the "cloud of witnesses" in the passage above.

The majority are individuals with less than stellar track records. It might be more appropriate to call Hebrews 11 the "hall of shame."

Take Abraham for example (Hebrews 11 v 8-19). The guy lied about being married to his wife so he could avoid personal danger. He seemed okay exposing his wife to potential harm. But at least he only did it once, right? Nope, he did it twice.

Check it out for yourself in Genesis chapters 12 and 20. And while you are at it, read chapter 26, where his son Isaac, who is also mentioned in the "hall of faith" (Hebrews 11 v 20), does the same thing to his wife. Is this the model example of living by faith?

The failings continue as we walk through the hall. Isaac's son, Jacob, lied to his dad to get the blessing that should have been his brother's (Genesis 27). Moses was used by God to rescue the Israelites from Egypt, yet was forbidden from entering the promised land because he had disobeyed God's command (Numbers 20 v 12). And Gideon ended up making a gold object that he and all the Israelites worshiped instead of God (Judges 8 v 22-27).

The "hall of faith" is covered with muddy footprints. It's not a sterile passageway. It's littered with messy lives: liars, idolaters, adulterers, cowards, and murderers. It's an untidy hallway. But it does lead somewhere…

Jesus: Our Better Way

At our house we have a mudroom when you enter the backdoor. It's where our kids take their shoes off before walking into the house. Hebrews 11 is something like a mudroom. We meet men and women who did some exemplary things by faith, even if their lives were inconsistent in other areas.

But we aren't meant to stop there. We have to enter the house. There's a meal sitting on the table, fresh coffee brewing, a pie in the oven, and a fire in the fireplace. We have to see beyond the mudroom to something better.

Fix your eyes on Jesus. That's what the author of Hebrews tells us. The real hero of Hebrews chapter eleven is found in chapter twelve. Everyone else falls short. I think that's the point. A theme throughout the book of Hebrews is that *Jesus is better*. Why should that theme stop with the hall of faith?

We see that Jesus faithfully walked the path God the Father ordained for him. He endured the cross, all the while scorning the shame (Hebrews 12 v 2). The cloud of witnesses is helpful. But Jesus is better. Jesus shows us how to follow God in the wild without compromise. Fix your eyes on him.

Are you tempted to feel a little better about your private sins after hearing about the moral inconsistencies among those listed in Hebrews chapter 11? If so, get ready for the challenge of chapter 12. Here we're told to throw off anything that holds us back from running in the way God has prepared for us.

Therefore, since we are surrounded by such a great cloud of witnesses, let us throw off everything that hinders and the sin that so easily entangles. (Hebrews 12 v 1)

The author of Hebrews mentions two things: (1) everything that hinders; and (2) the sin that so easily entangles. The first category isn't necessarily a moral judgment. It is contrasted with the mention of sin. So, we have to remove some potentially good things if they distract us.

Just as marathon runners don't compete in trench coats, so we must avoid unnecessary baggage if we are to run. Just as horses wear blinders when racing, so we have to develop a singular vision. We have to focus.

The second category—"the sin that so easily entangles"—is clearly moral. In the wild—where sin lurks in the shadows, crouching, waiting to pounce—we will find this to be a difficult command to obey. We have sins that seem so easily to become wrapped around our ankles. And if we trip, we find ourselves enmeshed in a web of iniquity.

For the person who has experienced a life-transforming encounter with Jesus, there is help. Jesus has promised that his Spirit will guide us in the way of all truth (John 16 v 13). That includes learning to walk again. In time he will teach us to run. But first we must get rid of some things and focus on what matters.

Listen and Learn

You will never regret anything you give up for Jesus. But you will regret everything you hold back. You can listen and learn—or you can live and learn. But we all must learn. There are no exceptions.

Experience is a painful guide. As the author C.S. Lewis once said:

Experience: that most brutal of teachers. But you learn, my God do you learn.

That's why the writer of Hebrews implores us to cast off sin and fix our eyes on Jesus. It's better to listen and learn than live and learn.

If we will listen, in Jesus we find an example for our lives and strength for our journey. With Jesus we are reminded that God's process of disciplining us, leading us to cast off sin, is motivated by his love for us as our Father (Hebrews 12 v 7-11).

This is a loving process, but it hurts like crazy. It's like spiritual chemotherapy. It won't feel like love in the moment.

But we must learn to embrace this painful process if we are to listen and learn.

Hebrews 12 emphasizes this point with the illustration of Esau, a man whose little brother is listed in Hebrews 11. Since he was the oldest son, it should have been Esau in the story that carried on the family's legacy of faith. But Esau traded his story, his birthright, his place in God's promises, to his little brother for a bowl of soup (Hebrews 12 v 16). You can read more about this Old Testament story in Genesis 25.

Like Esau, we face moments where we are presented with something that seems so appealing, so compelling—intoxicating even. And in those moments we make decisions that deeply affect the direction of our lives.

For Eve, it was a piece of forbidden fruit and the thought of possessing divine knowledge, deciding for herself what was good and not good. For Esau, it was a meal. What is it for you?

The good news is that God offers forgiveness for repentant rebels who have tried to rewrite his moral code. If we confess our sins, he is faithful to forgive us (1 John 1 v 9). The New Testament also tells us to confess our sins to one another and pray for one another (James 5 v 16). In Christ we find forgiveness and strength; and in community with brothers and sisters who are also fighting the battle of faith, we find accountability and support. It's here where we can learn to run.

Is this something you need to do now? If so, take the time to confess your sin to the Lord and ask his forgiveness. Will you confide in a trusted Christian brother or sister, and ask for their help and prayers? If so, who and when? Will you commit to living for God in the wild, and ask the Spirit to work in your life as you do so, showing you clearly what is good and what is not, so that the lines are no longer blurry?

Let the reader beware. Running in the wild is neither easy nor safe. But we have a faithful guide. You will hear the serpent's lie remixed to your favorite tune: "Did God really say?"

Yes. God did really say. And Jesus obeyed his word perfectly. So, fix your eyes on him.

CHAPTER 4
WAR OF THE WORLDS

"To the woman [God] said, 'I will make your pains in childbearing very severe; with painful labor you will give birth to children. Your desire will be for your husband, and he will rule over you.'"

GENESIS 3 v 16

Men and women are different. Back in Genesis chapters one and two this was easy and uncontroversial. But since the rebellion, even this has gotten confusing.

My aim in this chapter is simple. I hope to show that there is an original design for men and women, that we have fallen from this design, and that the path toward flourishing is found in returning to God's loving design.

There might be some parts of this chapter that will be difficult and perhaps even painful for some readers. The Bible brings both comfort and confrontation to all who take it seriously. I don't want to add to this. That's why I will do my best not to overstate or understate what the Bible says on these issues. Great damage can be found in either direction.

Genesis presents our gender roles as a loving gift to us from God. But we live in a fallen world where even our relationship to God's gifts is affected by the curse of sin.

The fall affected what it means to be a woman and what it means to be a man.

That's why I want to point to a simple and basic way that God has made the universe to work as revealed in the Bible—and how our pursuit of this as human beings can bring us joy, and how our rejection of it will bring us pain. Just as we cannot ignore the physical laws governing the universe, put there by God, neither can we ignore the moral laws.

Outside of Eden, none of this is going to come naturally. It's an uphill journey every step of the way. There are no shortcuts.

One Man's Irrelevant Thoughts on the Pain of Childbirth

In Genesis 3, God reveals how the fall will affect human beings and the world they live in.

He tells Eve:

> *I will make your pains in childbearing very severe; with*
> *painful labor you will give birth to children.*
> *(Genesis 3 v 16)*

I'm not sure what it would have been like for Eve to have a child before she and Adam rebelled against God. Would it have been pain-free? We cannot know, as she didn't have children until they were out of the garden.

The pain mentioned here initially applies to the act of giving birth. This is a topic on which I have no firsthand knowledge. My wife and I are the proud parents of four children: three stinky boys and one delightful and perfect little girl. We have three ogres and one princess.

All our children have been delivered through C-section. Being an eyewitness to these surgeries, I can say it looks terribly painful. I'm thankful I'm a dude. I'm the fourth ogre in our house, I suppose. We are *Smelly, Stink, Stank,* and *Stunk* living with a *Queen April* and *Princess Addilynn.*

I'm a wimp when it comes to blood. If I see even a little, I get a salty taste in my mouth and the world begins to sway off kilter.

Our anesthesiologist didn't appreciate my weak stomach. As they pulled Isaiah, our firstborn twin, from the incision in my wife's stomach, the anesthesiologist grabbed my hospital gown at the shoulder and fought to pull me up so I wouldn't miss this marvel of human achievement. I resisted. He persisted.

Finally my wife, who should have been focused on more important things, spoke up. "Please don't make him watch. He might pass out," she said. So I remained hidden behind the curtain that separated my wife and I from the surgery.

And then, from behind the curtain, a well-intentioned nurse jumped out, like a circus clown with a bit of a triumphant bounce, and held up a small humanlike figure covered in who knows what. I fell out of my chair onto the hospital floor. I'm told my last words before blacking out were, "Put it back!"

Just kidding. I survived. My wife was okay too. Thanks for asking.

But I will admit I was a little frightened at the first sight of our children. In the movies they come out clean, wrapped in swaddling cloths, cooing and smiling, covered in an angelic glow. Not our kids. They initially looked like blood-drenched aliens, something from a low-budget horror film. But they've improved greatly, I'm happy to say.

A Parent's Pain

In addition to the physical pain of childbirth, Eve faced the psychological pain of knowing her children would encounter a very different world than Eden. Bringing children into a scary world carries its own source of pain.

Adam and Eve's family story is sad and dark. Just read Genesis 4. I'm pretty sure Eve's pain in childbirth paled in comparison to what she and Adam experienced from their grown children, Cain and Abel.

We're not given a lot of details but what we see is horrifying. We are told that Cain and Abel both offered sacrifices to God. Cain grew up to be a farmer; Abel, a shepherd. Cain brought crops for an offering and Abel brought an animal. Here's the account:

> *Now Abel kept flocks, and Cain worked the soil. In the course of time Cain brought some of the fruits of the soil as an offering to the LORD. And Abel also brought an offering—fat portions from some of the firstborn of his flock. The LORD looked with favor on Abel and his offering, but on Cain and his offering he did not look with favor. So Cain was very angry, and his face was downcast.*

> *Then the LORD said to Cain, "Why are you angry? Why is your face downcast? If you do what is right, will you not be accepted? But if you do not do what is right, sin is crouching at your door; it desires to have you, but you must rule over it."*

Now Cain said to his brother Abel, "Let's go to the
field." While they were in the field, Cain attacked his
brother Abel and killed him. Then the LORD *said to*
Cain, "Where is your brother Abel?" "I don't know," he
replied. "Am I my brother's keeper?" (Genesis 4 v 2-9)

Don't forget: we're only a handful of verses away from Eden. So soon, we read of domestic violence and homicide in the headlines of human news. Too soon, we feel the full weight of our rebellion: our innocence left behind, hanging on a branch in the Garden of Eden.

Four chapters into the greatest book ever written, we find the first human brothers separated by anger, envy, and finally murder. The third person to breathe air on our planet killed the fourth.

This shows that outside of Eden there is no "golden age." There is a whole lot of pain surrounding a promise that one day God will make all things good again.

This battle, this human struggle, is a part of a cosmic conflict with God's design. Part of our resistance is because no one wants to be crammed into what they fear is a cookie-cutter mold. All of us want a little leeway to figure out who we are and who we want to be. And even if we accept that God's design is best, it still can sometimes feel like an intrusion on our personal liberty.

Gender Within Community

We don't live out our lives in isolation. We were never intended to. Who we are, and who we're becoming, happens in the context of community. God designed us to live before him in a right relationship, but he also made us to live in right relationships with others.

This means that God's gift of gender is not just for the individual but also for the community. God has made us male and female for each other. It is a shared gift. It is the fabric of society.

God doesn't just show us gender roles in isolation, like separate instruction manuals for men and women, but gives us a picture of the gender roles in relationship with one another. These roles are given human examples, in Genesis through the *family*, and then additionally, through the account of the *church* in the New Testament.

Confusion, disobedience, and selfishness toward others prevent us from experiencing the beauty of God's design.

It can get confusing. Maybe that's why God keeps things so basic in Genesis. He doesn't give us many details: just seemingly minor references to the roles of being man and woman. But what's there is surely important.

Much of what we can learn about the family in Genesis comes to us in a negative fashion. In the first two chapters of Genesis we see the importance of the husband-and-wife relationship and its role in populating the earth. What we learn after chapter 3 is often from the perspective of the fall. We are seeing reflections of what should have been, but we're looking through a shattered mirror.

We strain to see God's design through the broken lives in the Bible and from the vantage point of our own brokenness. Ask any adult about the dysfunction they experienced growing up, no matter how happy their childhood was, and they will have many examples of pain and disappointment. Talk to any successful married couple and they will tell you that marriage is hard work.

Misplaced Desires

Becoming who God wants us to be, and living this out in community with others, isn't easy. We are all broken people. And it's in this brokenness that God tells Eve that the first couple will default to using their gender roles in selfish ways:

> *Your desire will be for your husband, and he will rule over you. (Genesis 3 v 16)*

It's interesting that Eve's *desire* would be for her husband. I don't think God is speaking of sexual desire here. Sex isn't a part of the curse. It isn't a result of sin. God designed sex and blessed it *before* the fall.

So, if this isn't referring to sexual desire, what is it talking about? To answer this we need to look deeper into Genesis. There is an interesting parallel in Genesis 4. Look at the similarities of these two passages, the first directed to Eve and the second to Cain:

> To Eve: *"Your **desire** will be for your husband, and he will **rule** over you." (Genesis 3 v 16, bold text mine)*

> To Cain: *"If you do not do what is right, sin is crouching at your door; it **desires** to have you, but you must **rule** over it." (Genesis 4 v 7, bold text mine)*

Before Cain kills his brother Abel, God explains to him that sin *desires* him but he must *rule* over it (Genesis 4 v 7). Sin wants to master him. Cain must master sin instead. He must not let sin have its way.

In context, God's words to Eve imply that she will desire to rule over Adam, to master him. That doesn't fit the original description of Eve being created as a *helper* (Genesis 2 v 18). But Adam doesn't respond the way he should either. Eve is told that Adam will rule over her.

The notion of Adam *ruling over* Eve doesn't fit the New Testament teaching that a man should love his wife as Christ loved the church (Ephesians 5 v 25). Adam is seeking to rule over Eve in the way Cain was told to rule over sin.

We must be careful how we view these effects. God is not saying to Eve, "You did wrong, so it is okay for Adam to treat you poorly." God is explaining a new reality that will affect their marriage in a fallen world. This is the result of sin, the consequence of disobedience. The first couple would now struggle to live out God's good design for their lives as individuals and as a family.

The challenges they face—that we all face—come in various forms but can be traced back to the same problem: a failure to live out God's design. We are impacted by our own sins and the sins of others. Whether in the forms of male chauvinism, radical feminism, or a rejection of the categories of gender altogether, as broken people living with the effects of sin even followers of Jesus will struggle to live out God's design for ourselves and our communities.

The impact of sin shakes the foundation of what it means to made male and female in the image of God, and in turn, shakes the foundation of society. In the wild, Eve's desire would be for Adam. She would squirm under the biblical title assigned to her of *helper*. And Adam would make it worse. Instead of being a servant leader, he would resort to being a dictator.

Bad Leadership

Caution is in order here. We must not reject God's original intent because of abuses. The New Testament authors certainly didn't. The apostle Paul points back to the goodness of God's original design for the family and applies it to the church.

In the New Testament, we discover that appointed men were to serve the church as loving shepherds, as elders and pastors. Paul bases this model on the creation account:

> *I do not permit a woman to teach or to assume*
> *authority over a man ... For Adam was formed first,*
> *then Eve. (1 Timothy 2 v 12-13)*

But sadly, as with the first family, even in the church we find men who misuse their leadership position. The apostle Peter addresses this when he says:

> *To the elders among you, I appeal as a fellow elder*
> *... Be shepherds of God's flock that is under your*
> *care, watching over them ... not lording it over those*
> *entrusted to you, but being examples to the flock.*
> *(1 Peter 5 v 1-3)*

The New Testament model for pastoral leadership further illustrates what we find in Genesis. Biological gender is not a coincidence or an accident, but an intentional design for individuals, for the home, and for the church. Men are to love their wives as Jesus loves the church, and wives are to follow their husbands as though they are following Jesus (Ephesians 5 v 22, 25).

But in the wild there is a whole lot going on that doesn't look like Jesus. There's a lot of *desiring* and a lot of *ruling*. It's a hot mess. And we're all part of it.

Love. Don't Judge.

That's why it shouldn't really surprise us to find other forms of cultural confusion over gender. If these categories are confused and abused in the church, how can we expect those outside the church to see the beauty of God's design?

Several years ago I started and led a new meeting location for our local church in Louisville, Kentucky. The church had seven different locations throughout our city where our members could worship. The meeting I led was at the University of Louisville.

We met in the "Red Barn." It was neither red nor a barn. That's simply what they called it. It was a stand-alone building in the middle of campus that had a large gathering room and one office annex. We shared the building with the LGBTQ office that was located in the front corner, connected by a hallway with common restrooms.

The first book of the Bible I preached a series through was Romans. I remember teaching through the first chapter of Paul's letter on that Sunday evening. Coincidentally, it was also the kick-off night for Gay Pride Week at the school. That made for something of a crosscurrent of worldviews in the Red Barn.

I ended my talk with the sins the apostle Paul outlines that result from rejecting God's design. If you've read Romans, you know this is an often-referred-to section of Scripture dealing with homosexuality (Romans 1 v 26-27). But Paul's list of sins doesn't end there. The list includes *gossip, greed, envy, murder, strife, deceit, malice, slander, hating God, arrogance, boasting,* and *being disobedient to parents.*

When we came out of worship that night, we discovered that someone had drawn a large rainbow in chalk on the sidewalk in front of the building. I don't remember the exact words but it was something to the effect of, "Love. Don't Judge."

Would it surprise you if I told you I agreed?

I think reading Romans shows us that we are *all* on the list. While sexual sins have a pronounced place in the passage, it's clear none of us are without blame. I'm guessing, if nothing else, that we've all disobeyed our parents at one time or another. My hunch is you've been guilty of a couple of the other sins on the list too. I know I have.

Paul's list should stir both conviction and empathy within every one of us. We're all guilty. We're all broken. Sure, we can point to sins on the list that don't apply to us, but what about the ones we are guilty of? This may be a good moment to stop, read again the list of sins above, and come to the Lord with honest repentance.

God has a design—and human flourishing can be found in pursuing this design. We all need grace. None of us will survive in the wild simply because we are that good on our own. It's too messy and too broken for any of us to be able to pull this off without divine help.

We have to admit we can't fix ourselves. We must return to God's design. The word in the Bible that describes this is *repentance*. It means recognizing we've deviated from God's ways and that we want to come back. And the good news is, for all of us, whoever or wherever we are, that God will, like the father of the prodigal son (Luke 15 v 20), welcome us home with open arms.

But this won't be easy. In fact, without God's help we cannot do it. But that's good news too: God has promised us help. The Bible doesn't command us to change first and then come to

Christ, but to come to Christ as we are. And Christ has promised to give us his Spirit to live inside us and help us begin the process of becoming who God created us to be (2 Corinthians 3 v 18). As the Christian author Max Lucado has said, "God loves us where we are, but he loves us too much to let us stay there."

The War Within

I recognize that some may not only struggle to see and be convinced of the biblical roles for men and women, but might have a deeper reservation. They might struggle with the notion of a pre-assigned gender altogether. Some may experience what is called "gender dysphoria"—the feeling of not identifying with their biological gender.

This is too big a topic to try to tackle in one chapter, let alone one part of a chapter. I would recommend anyone wanting a kind yet biblical response to consider Vaughan Roberts' book *Transgender*. He encourages believers who are thinking about this subject with these words:

> *We need to begin by remembering that we are not simply talking about "issues" here, but people: precious individuals, each created and loved by God. Most of them don't have a strong political agenda or any desire to fight in a "culture war"; they are simply trying to cope with feelings that may well cause them great distress.*

Our biological gender is a gift from God. But in the wild we are at war with ourselves, even with our own bodies. As I've heard Christian author, speaker, and friend, Sam Allberry, point out, every person has some degree of brokenness related to their relationship with their body.

I once heard another ministry leader explain that everyone north of puberty understands disordered sexual desires. That's because we all—heterosexual, same-sex-attracted, homosexual, or transgender—struggle with degrees of brokenness in regards to our identity and our sexuality.

There is a civil war inside our chests.

Since Genesis, men and women have found it difficult to make peace with God's design. This age-old divide is illustrated in the title of the bestselling book from the 1990s: *Men are From Mars, Women are From Venus*. To expand this planetary metaphor, another book title, one from the 1890s, illustrates our contemporary challenge: *The War of the Worlds*.

Mars and Venus are at war. There is war without. There is war within. We all feel it.

It reminds me of the country-music song title, "Bless the Broken Road." There is a path to life for broken people like you and me. Sin desires to keep us from it. Not many will find or travel on it. But though our companions will be few, flourishing is found on the narrow road that leads us straight to him.

Will you join me? We will take it slow. Just take one step at a time.

CHAPTER 5

IT'S NOT EASY BEING GREEN

"By the sweat of your brow you will eat your food until you return to the ground, since from it you were taken; for dust you are and to dust you will return."

GENESIS 3 V 19

L iving in the wild isn't easy. No one said it would be— and God never said it should be. The original couple experienced a severed relationship with God, their relationship with one another was taxed, and (as we'll see in this chapter) their relationship with the land was strained. That's not an ideal formula for flourishing. We've been living in this soup ever since.

That's why survival tactics have been necessary since Genesis 3. The publishing world understands this. They provide an A–Z of survival books, from Animal attacks to the Zombie apocalypse.

I doubt survival guides will ever go out of style while we inhabit this fallen planet. We're all suckers for finding a way to stay alive.

Even the religious would rather avoid death. As the title of one jazz song says, "Everybody wants to go to heaven, but nobody wants to die." Scientific theories focus on survival too. The widely accepted theory of evolution seems to be based on "survival of the fittest."

But is the survival of our species enough?

We're Not in Kansas Anymore

Is mere existence enough to get us out of bed every morning? The stories we hear of perseverance in the face of death are rarely just about staying alive another day—they focus on some higher purpose such as family, friends, or unfinished life goals. So what higher aims can motivate us to grit our teeth and press forward when things get really tough?

The Bible addresses this question. It speaks where science is silent. While science gives us *survival of the fittest*, Scripture gives a foundation for the things that make survival worth pursuing. Better put, the Bible shows us a life worth living.

Most survival guides deal with two basic things: understanding a dangerous situation, and finding a way out without dying. My goal in this chapter is a little more ambitious. I think the Bible gives us more than a map to survival. I believe it shows us how to *thrive* in the wild.

The Bible can help us understand the world and our place in it. The first thing it does is to help us get our bearings for life outside of the garden. What should we expect in the wild? Genesis gives us some broad categories for making sense of our dangerous situation in the natural world.

What we find in Genesis regarding nature is pretty basic. The animals are now cursed (Genesis 3 v 14) and so is the land

(Genesis 3 v 17). We might skim over these statements about the results of our rebellion. We shouldn't.

Stop and think about it for a moment. We live in a world that is cursed and we're surrounded by animals that are cursed. *Lions and tigers and bears, oh my!* It's simply not safe in the wild.

Christians who take the Bible seriously shouldn't have their faith undone when they hear of tsunamis or animal attacks. We live in a cursed creation and we're surrounded by cursed critters. Walt Disney might have popularized singing animals and the song, "It's a Small World (After All)," but don't be fooled. It may be a small world, relatively speaking, but it's a small, scary world.

That's maybe why Adam is told he will labor by the sweat of his brow outside the garden in the midst of thorns and thistles:

> *To Adam [God] said, "Because you listened to your wife*
> *and ate fruit from the tree about which I commanded*
> *you, 'You must not eat from it,'*
>
> *"Cursed is the ground because of you;*
> *   through painful toil you will eat food from it*
> *   all the days of your life.*
> *It will produce thorns and thistles for you,*
> *   and you will eat the plants of the field.*
> *By the sweat of your brow*
> *   you will eat your food*
> *until you return to the ground,*
> *   since from it you were taken;*
> *for dust you are*
> *   and to dust you will return." (Genesis 3 v 17-19)*

Perspiration surely wasn't new. Adam had worked in Eden. But in the wild he'd experience a cold sweat.

He'd be working the land while the land was working him. While he was looking for something to eat, there'd be something looking to eat him. Like going for a late-night snack to discover your refrigerator has grown teeth.

The biblical picture of living in the wild is a constant sense of not belonging. We're exiles—and this foreign country isn't friendly.

That's why I'm surprised when I hear skeptics point to natural evil as a demonstration that Christianity isn't true. That reveals a serious ignorance of the full biblical storyline including the fall. Believers, above all people, should expect natural disasters. Scripture is big enough to make sense of sinkholes and shark bites.

A Terrible Beauty

But there's also something terribly beautiful about the world. From the Grand Canyon to the Caribbean islands, it seems like a wonderful world after all. How do we fight for faith on a planet that is filled with both wonder and horror?

C.S. Lewis once described it this way: "Nature has all the air of a good thing spoiled."

It's true that the earth is under a curse. A theology of the world—a biblical view of the cosmos—helps us make sense of what we see in the headlines and out of our windows every day. Understanding our position in this fallen place can help put things in perspective.

Contrast the beauty of the world with some of the natural disasters in just the last century or so. In the early 1930s, the Republic of China faced the worst flooding in their history. Some estimate that over three million lives were lost in a series of devastating floods. Millions more were made homeless and lost virtually all their possessions.

Four decades later the Chinese people suffered what many consider to be the worst earthquake of the twentieth century. Hundreds of thousands were severely injured or killed.

The day after Christmas, two years in a row, horror ravaged thousands. On December 26, 2003, central Iran faced an earthquake that claimed tens of thousands of lives. Many victims were crushed to death while still sleeping.

One year later, on December 26, 2004, the tide receded along the coast of Sumatra, India. A video of people visiting the beach shows them standing in amazement as the water seems to disappear to the horizon. An undersea earthquake caused the Indian Ocean at first to pull back and then to surge forward. Waves as high as one hundred feet (30m) hit over a dozen countries like a massive wrecking ball. Over two-hundred thousand people died.

But earthquakes and tsunamis aren't the only things to worry about in the wild. Nature is alive. We aren't alone.

We're surrounded by things that would love to maul us. A good friend recently experienced this in a horrific way when a neighbor's dog attacked his young daughter, nearly biting the nose off her face. After multiple reconstructive surgeries she's as beautiful as ever, but it's a powerful illustration of the effects of the fall on the natural world.

And sometimes the things we need to fear most don't bark or growl. Mosquitoes are the deadliest creatures on our planet, causing over one million deaths per year.

Genesis leads us to expect all of these things. That doesn't make it any easier, but Christians need not think that natural evil contradicts the biblical story. It *illustrates* it. The biblical doctrine of the fall anticipates earthquakes, tsunamis, and malaria-spreading mosquitoes.

The apostle Paul explains that Adam and Eve were not the only ones who experienced disastrous effects because of the rebellion. God responded by putting all of creation under a curse. And, like humanity, creation itself longs for redemption:

I consider that our present sufferings are not worth comparing with the glory that will be revealed in us. For the creation waits in eager expectation for the children of God to be revealed. For the creation was subjected to frustration, not by its own choice, but by the will of the one who subjected it, in hope that the creation itself will be liberated from its bondage to decay and brought into the freedom and glory of the children of God. We know that the whole creation has been groaning as in the pains of childbirth right up to the present time.
(Romans 8 v 18-22)

The big story of the Bible is that God made a good creation that he then put under a curse because of our rebellion—and that he has promised to one day make all things good again. That's why Paul later says, "And we know that in all things God works for the good of those who love him, who have been called according to his purpose" (Romans 8 v 28). All of creation longs for God to restore goodness.

What Is Our Place in This Fallen World?
Reflecting on the effects of the fall won't fill you with a warm sense of nostalgia. It's a harsh reality. It's more like a child from a broken family thinking back to her parents' divorce. It's not

pretty. Because of human sinfulness, we were ripped from the home we loved. Now we live in the midst of brokenness.

What does the Bible say about humanity's place in this fallen world? Do we have any worth outside of Eden? How should we understand ourselves and our place?

King David dealt with similar questions. Look at what he says about the relationship of humanity to God and the world:

When I consider your heavens,
*   the work of your fingers,*
the moon and the stars,
*   which you have set in place,*
what is mankind *that you are mindful of them,*
*   human beings that you care for them?*

You have made them a little lower than the angels
*   and crowned them with glory and honor.*
You made them rulers over the works of your hands;
*   you put everything under their feet:*
all flocks and herds,
*   and the animals of the wild,*
the birds in the sky,
*   and the fish in the sea,*
*   all that swim the paths of the seas.*
(Psalm 8 v 3-8, bold text mine)

In answering the question, "What is mankind?" David looks back to the creation account in Genesis. Why would he do that? Why would he go back to Eden to define our worth? We don't live in the garden any more.

You might think that because of our rebellion we've lost all intrinsic value. But that's not the case. David goes back to the

Genesis account because the things that give creation worth were established *before* the rebellion. Our purpose, and that of creation, may seem blurred or distorted because of the effects of the curse, but it is still there. God's intentions for us and our world haven't changed.

Honor and Worth

Psalm 8 shows us that humans still have great honor. We have deep-seated worth from God. We also have important responsibilities. We are to care for God's world. Both humanity and nature still have great value to God. We are made a little lower than the angels—and all creation is placed under our feet (Psalm 8 v 5).

Humanity is the apex of creation. This has been God's design from the beginning:

> *Then God said, "Let us make mankind in our image,*
> *in our likeness, so that they may rule over the fish in the*
> *sea and the birds in the sky, over the livestock and all the*
> *wild animals, and over all the creatures that move along*
> *the ground." (Genesis 1 v 26)*

Adam and Eve were to serve as God's representatives to extend his rule over the world. As sons and daughters of Adam and Eve, we share this identity and this responsibility.

God is the author of creation and the one who determines human worth. That's why the sermons and speeches of the abolitionists who fought to end the slave trade are filled with references to the creation account in Genesis. Human equality makes sense if we are *created equal.*

If we merely happen to be the species that is the *most fit for survival,* then there isn't much objective worth. There is only brute force. But human equality based on God's design means that every human being has true worth from the weakest to the strongest, from the least of these to the greatest.

The founding fathers of America expressed this when they wrote:

> *We hold these truths to be self-evident, that all men are created equal, that they are endowed by their Creator with certain unalienable Rights.*

Our Creator gave his creation certain rights and responsibilities that were not undone by the fall. They are "unalienable," which means they cannot be alienated, or separated, from humanity.

In his book *Genesis in Space and Time*, the late Christian writer Francis Schaeffer explains how humanity has not lost its intrinsic worth as a result of the fall:

> *Man's sin causes all these separations between man and God, man and himself, man and man, and man and nature … But there is one thing which he did not lose, and that is his **mannishness**, his being a human being. Man still stands in the image of God—twisted, broken, abnormal, but still the image-bearer of God. Man did not stop being human.*

Adam and Eve did not stop being human when they were forced to leave the garden. They were still God's image-bearers. Like Adam and Eve, we sit at the top of the food chain with a command to care for creation. We share in Adam and Eve's job of ruling and subduing creation for its good and for God's glory. That's a pretty large order.

Going Green

God has entrusted humans with the care of the planet. Our intrinsic worth is connected to our great responsibility. The biblical perspective on humanity and creation keeps us from two extremes—either worshiping nature or seeing it merely as a resource to be exploited. The earth is a gift to be both treasured and developed.

But the biblical perspective takes us further still. Jesus' command to love our neighbor (Mark 12 v 31) has serious implications for how we live on this planet. This means Christians must take into account both our stewardship of the earth and our love for our neighbor. We cannot rule and subdue nature at the expense of nature, for it is a gift—or at the expense of our neighbor, whom we are called to love.

So Christians have to give great thought to how best to steward the earth in a way that cares for the people God loves. We cannot misuse the earth simply because we know it will one day cease to exist (when God makes a new heaven and earth, Isaiah 65 v 17; Revelation 21 v 1). Just because something will not last forever doesn't mean it should be neglected or abused. Can you imagine someone leaving his or her child with a babysitter who holds that view?

Christians should give careful thought to matters to do with the environment. Believers might disagree on controversial issues ranging from climate change to coal mining. What we cannot do is see these as trivial. We must take our God-given care of the planet seriously, for ourselves and our neighbors living downstream.

So stop for a moment and ask yourself when you last gave thought to environmental issues. And whether you looked at them through biblical eyes. If your answer shows that it was long ago, or more of a response to eco-warriors than biblical viewpoints, set aside some time to give this some thought. And ask God to help you respond in a way that both honors him and points those around you to the loving Creator, who made and sustains our world.

A Christian View of Ecology

Several years ago I was part of a ministry team serving on a secular university campus. Our team planned and led an event called "Is God Green? A Christian View of Ecology." For promotion, we passed out eco-friendly shopping bags branded with the event details.

Out of all our seminars, this one led to the most confusion. "Christians care about the environment?" students seemed to say with their expressions when they read the words printed on the bag. While the title "Is God Green?" was more of an attention-grabber, it was the idea of a Christian view of ecology that had the most intrigue.

This was also one of the least controversial topics we covered. Not because we didn't give a clear biblical presentation. We did. We explained the Christian view of seeing creation as a gift as a better model than seeing the world as a mere accident. While many of the non-religious students disagreed with our argument, they seemed delightfully surprised to hear Christians talking about concern and care for the planet.

Caring for Creation While Living in the Wild

Is this because Christians haven't been vocal enough about our view of creation? Maybe that's why some skeptics feel that natural disasters disprove the Christian message. It could be that Christians have not taken what the Bible says about nature seriously enough or talked about it clearly.

We must fight for faith by looking to Scripture to understand our world and our place in it. Admittedly, it can be scary living in the wild. It's filled with volcanoes and vultures. Our theology leads us to expect the fallen world to be wild. But our theology also points to a time when all will be made new.

For the meantime, we are called to live in this wild place. And though we may be a long way from Eden, we aren't left without hope or meaning. We are endowed with worth, rights, and responsibilities. God has entrusted us with the care of the earth—and as we care for it, we not only please him but also find opportunities to point non-believers to the Creator, who made and sustains it.

But as we'll see in the next chapter, life in the wild gets even worse. We're living in enemy-occupied territory. Everything we care about and work for is under attack by something unnatural. Even as I write this, and at this very moment as you read it, there is a war all around us. Fighting for faith is going to be harder than we may realize.

CHAPTER 6

THE DEVIL TO PAY

"So the LORD God said to the serpent, 'Because you have done this, Cursed are you above all livestock and all wild animals! You will crawl on your belly and you will eat dust all the days of your life. And I will put enmity between you and the woman, and between your offspring and hers; he will crush your head, and you will strike his heel.'"

GENESIS 3 V 14-15

I f we could see this evil with our own eyes, it would scare the hell out of us. Literally. If we understood the darkness in our world, the wicked undertones inherent within every temptation, the spiritual warfare surrounding every decision we make, the cloud of depravity always whirling, like storm clouds, just overhead—it would make us all want to live differently.

But we're far too sophisticated to talk about such things. This is to our own peril. Thinking people don't really believe in demons and Satan and evil. Except for when we do. Such as when there is a terrorist attack, or a young girl is abducted, or a teenager goes on a shooting spree.

No, at these times everyone, the religious and unreligious alike, employ the same kind of moral language. In moments of terror, we all believe in evil. It's strange, isn't it? With all of our advances in science, medicine, and technology—with all of our culture, literature, and art—at bottom, we still believe in the devil.

That's because our world is steeped in spiritual struggle. If we are to make it in the wild, we will have to find an explanation of the world that is big enough to include evil. It will not surprise you that I believe this is best found in a Christian view of reality.

Seeing Past the Veil of Familiarity

In Western culture, it can be difficult to talk about demons without feeling embarrassed. If we discuss spiritual warfare in public, we probably lower our voices. If someone interrupts our conversation, we will likely change the subject so they don't think we are fanatics. Why do you think this is so?

We might get a better idea of the spiritual realities of our world by looking at the stories that captivate our culture's attention. Ask yourself why stories such as J.R.R. Tolkien's famous *The Lord of the Rings* trilogy capture our attention.

In 2003, the BBC named *The Lord of the Rings* as Britain's best-loved book. A year later, the film version was ranked as Australia's favorite film, beating *Star Wars*. Why do you think we're so enthralled with Tolkien's stories of hobbits, elves, ghouls, a ring, and an all-seeing eye?

I think it's because these stories illustrate a battle between light and darkness that reflects something real in our own world. Even though we cannot physically see this spiritual warfare, as in Tolkien's Middle-earth, we *feel* it. In our inner being, deep down, many of us believe it to be real. We sense it, and we fear that this moral sense is to be trusted.

The apostle Paul described this reality:

> *For our struggle is not against flesh and blood, but against the rulers, against the authorities, against the powers of this dark world and against the spiritual forces of evil in the heavenly realms. (Ephesians 6 v 12)*

This is an accurate depiction of our fallen planet. We are fighting against the powers of darkness. And we will not win on our own.

Epic tales like Tolkien's are timeless because they echo our moral intuitions. They give vision to our inner sense of the way things really are. They provide a window of insight into the nature of our world.

C.S. Lewis, a friend of Tolkien, describes this well. In his review of *The Lord of the Rings* he explains how Tolkien is able to use myth to shed light on reality:

> *The value of myth is that it takes all the things we know and restores to them the rich significance which has been hidden by the "veil of familiarity."*

This *veil of familiarity,* which Lewis refers to, is the way we are numbed to spiritual realities if we only focus on what can be immediately seen. If we can't see something, we tend to ignore it. Out of sight, out of mind. But powerful stories, and sadly, horrific events in our own world, bring the spiritual struggle quickly back to the center.

"The utterly new achievement of Professor Tolkien," Lewis wrote, "is that he carries a comparable sense of reality unaided." By the term *reality unaided* Lewis is referring to the innate human understanding that we live in a moral universe, where good and evil are real. This is our unaided view of reality. We naturally see the world this way. We may try to hide this belief, but if we're squeezed, if we're scared, or backed into a corner, we often employ moral categories of good and evil because we know they're not illusions but the real framework of the world in which we live.

May the Force Be with You

Consider another famous saga. The *Star Wars* movies capitalize on audiences cheering for light to triumph over darkness. But as exciting as the films are—and believe me, I'm a fan—the plot is built around a contradiction.

Creator George Lucas implemented elements of Buddhist thought into the plot with his idea of the Force. He portrays the Force as a unifying spirit that permeates all things. But this doesn't really fit with the good-guys-versus-bad-guys motif.

Here's why: Buddhism teaches that all is one. "I am one with the Force and the Force is with me," repeats a character in the latest *Star Wars* story, *Rogue One*. But on this view, evil, if it is anything, is just a part of the oneness of the universe. If we take that perspective to its logical conclusion, then good and evil are basically the same thing.

We know better.

Any way of explaining the human experience that doesn't account for evil is fatally deficient. Evil is too prevalent and has too powerful an impact on our lives to be ignored or explained away.

How would you like a way of seeing the world—a worldview—that is big enough to make sense out of evil? You can find it in the Christian explanation of reality as outlined in the Bible.

Reading the Bible leads me to expect to find evil in the world; to expect an unraveling of the creation until a future point when God returns to make things good again. They will not get better on their own. The church is to play a vital role in the in-between time, but make no mistake: evil will not be undone by human efforts. We are doomed without divine intervention.

The Cadence of Providence

This is what God pledged Adam and Eve in the garden. He promised to intervene. He said he would send a child to defeat the serpent (the reptile form taken by Satan to deceive the first couple).

These words must have seemed odd to Adam and Eve, as they heard God tell the serpent:

> *I will put enmity between you and the woman, and between your offspring and hers; he will crush your head, and you will strike his heel. (Genesis 3 v 15)*

In time, a child of Eve would trade blows with the serpent—a bruised heel for a crushed skull. This would be a timely and costly remedy for the human rebellion.

The entire Bible is about this promise—the anticipation, fulfillment, and results of this serpent-crushing child. Christians understand this promise to refer to Jesus.

But this promise was not quickly fulfilled from a human perspective. Many generations would pass from the first couple before the promised child would arrive.

The apostle Paul explains that it happened at the perfect moment in heaven's economy of time—what Christians refer to as *providence*.

> *But when the set time had fully come, God sent his Son.*
> *(Galatians 4 v 4)*

I can't read the words "set time" without immediately thinking of a watch or a clock. Surely heaven has no need of such human devices, right? What exactly do you think heaven keeps time with to determine when the set time had fully come?

In one sense (since God is eternal and outside of time and space), we can say that heaven keeps time with human history. In that way, we're heaven's timepiece. What happens here is established by what is set there. Human history marches to the cadence of providence.

When the clock, or in this case, history, hit the preordained hour, God sent his Son. The Word became flesh (John 1 v 14). God crossed the threshold of time and space. At the right moment in time, the eternal Son of God entered this fallen little planet filled with rebels and curses and sin and death. He was born of a woman to rescue people like you and me.

In the spiritual realm, to Satan and his legion of demons, I'm sure this had to be seen as the most destructive event they had ever encountered. Maybe to them it looked like an atomic bomb descending from heaven, with a mushroom cloud rising over Bethlehem, sending shock waves around the world, rocking their evil power to the core. Maybe it was like a tsunami, with hope receding to the horizon for centuries only to come back in full force—waves hundreds of feet high, sending demonic despair reeling.

However it looked in the spiritual realm, we know what it must have been like in real life. It looked like seven pounds of human flesh wrapped in a first-century diaper. It reminds me of the animated Disney movie *Aladdin,* where the genie laments his condition. "Phenomenal cosmic power," he says, "Itty-bitty living space."

We know the angels responded to this scene with praise. "Glory to the God in the highest heaven, and on earth peace to those on whom his favor rests," they announced to shepherds keeping watch over their flocks at night (Luke 2 v 14).

I wonder if the demons sang a dirge in response, trying to drown out the heavenly choir. I imagine them keeping rhythm by pounding their "pitchforks" on the earth. Maybe their song went something like this:

This foul night, this foul night
In flesh now he has come

This burning, blistering light
In flesh now he has come

To steal men from our prison gate
For darkness we will fight till late

And take our stand, a cruel command
Christ to become the slaughtered lamb

Our gates, our gates, they must prevail
To keep men from the inner veil

Our gates, our gates, they must prevail
To keep men from the inner veil

A cross, a cross: we'll send him to a cross
'Tis not lost, a cross: we'll send him to the cross

Our gates, our gates, they must prevail
Our gates, our gates, they must prevail

Lest Christmas light, now shining bright,
Drive our souls to hell

The apostle John says that the Son of God appeared "to destroy the devil's work" (1 John 3 v 8). On that blessed night, heaven descended to earth, the groaning creation let out a sigh, and the serpent recoiled. Jesus' arrival made it clear that Satan's days, like time itself, were numbered.

After much ado, this Son of Eve came to make good on a promise made in a garden. This cosmic conflict would one day lead the child to a bloody cross, and the serpent to a desperate attack. Satan wasn't going out without a fight, and he would take as many prisoners as possible.

The Earthly Intermission

In the human theater, we are living between divine acts. In plays, the divisions of acts are often marked by major transitions in the plot. So in *The Phantom of the Opera*, the play begins with an auction where a shattered chandelier is on sale. The chandelier, an important piece in the story, rises to its original position, time rolls back, and the first act begins. At the end of the first act, the chandelier comes crashing down and the curtain closes. This definitive event divides the play and introduces the second act.

Similarly, the incarnation (God the Son born in human flesh) marks, from a worldly perspective, what seems like a massive plot twist. The curtain has closed on the Old Testament and the New Testament opens with the birth of God's Son. God entering time and space in the incarnation introduced a massive change in the story. Even history is marked by what preceded and what follows this event.

But another seismic plot change is in store. The drama isn't over yet. The final curtain call is yet to come.

We know from Scripture that Jesus will return in a similar way to the way he ascended into heaven (Acts 1 v 11). His visible and bodily return will bring an end to Satan's temporary rule. We live in the period of struggle and suffering between Jesus' earthly accomplishments and his future return—the final act of human history.

In the fullness of time God sent his Son. In the fullness of time he will send him again. This has been his plan all along. He stands outside of time and sees the end from the beginning. We stand somewhere in-between trying to make sense of it all. But we have his word, the Bible, as our guide.

Furthermore, God has not left us without comfort as we try to follow Jesus in the wild. Consider what the apostle Paul says in Galatians 4:

> *But when the set time had fully come, God sent his Son, born of a woman, born under the law, to redeem those under the law, that we might receive adoption to sonship. Because you are his sons, God sent the Spirit of his Son into our hearts, the Spirit who calls out, "Abba, Father." (Galatians 4 v 4-6)*

Not only did the Father send the Son at the appointed time; he also sent the Spirit. The Spirit of God fills those who trust in Christ and enables them to become more like Jesus through a process the Bible calls *sanctification*:

> *But you were washed, you were sanctified, you were justified in the name of the Lord Jesus Christ and by the Spirit of our God. (1 Corinthians 6 v 11)*

God is doing something beautiful in the lives of those who trust him. That's why the apostle Paul describes those who follow Jesus as God's handiwork or masterpiece (Ephesians 2 v 10). In the midst of this fallen and cursed world, God is putting his grace on display.

Welcome to the Moon

Several years ago I helped with a youth camp that had a theme of "Earth Tourists: This World Is Not Our Home." The stage was built to look like the moon, with a massive banner stretched across the back that looked as if you were in space gazing on the earth.

I was designated to design and build a UFO, the final touch to complete the set. I purchased several items from a local retail store and fashioned them into the most hillbilly spaceship you've ever seen. I used two kids' swimming pools, a clear beach ball, two ten-gallon buckets, swimming noodles, and a ton of chrome spray paint. No self-respecting alien would be caught dead flying this thing.

We hung it from the rafters with four lines of fishing string. Because of the banner on the back of the stage, it looked like the UFO was flying from the moon to the earth. It was spectacular, in my humble but accurate opinion.

But during the first camp service, one of the strings snapped.

The praise band leading worship didn't notice because they were facing the crowd. But the hundreds of teenagers before them became more than a little distracted by my UFO jittering on its departure for space.

I hoped they would think it was a planned effect. Hey kids, get ready for camp! We're going to the moon! It's going to be awesome!

To be honest, I began praying like crazy. I faked some inner peace to help me endure the moments to come. I resolved that this was God's will for my UFO. Instead of four cords holding it up, there were now only three. Kind of like the Trinity. Three was surely better than four. Surely God would uphold my UFO.

Snap. Another string broke. My UFO was now wobbling. Unfortunately the praise leader misinterpreted the commotion. The more the UFO moved, the more the audience reacted, and the more the band thought this was some form of spiritual awakening. It was a hot mess.

I began praying for Jesus to come back. Like, that very moment. That's the really big promise that Christians run to in moments of desperation. "Please protect my UFO," I repeated over and over, "or come back and take us all home."

Snap. The third string broke. My UFO was now swinging like a hypnotist's timepiece. There were hundreds of teenage heads swaying side to side as if they were watching a tennis match. The band was on the verge of a charismatic fit as they thought revival was spreading through the crowd like wildfire.

Snap. When the fourth string broke, my UFO rolled across the stage, hit an old piano, and exploded into a pile of junk. Swimming pools, noodles, buckets and a beach ball all toppled into the air, and then bounced across the platform in different directions.

On Display

As silly as this story might be, I do have a point. I didn't create the UFO to be a pile of junk on the side of the stage. I made it to be on display.

That's what God is doing in the lives of those who follow Jesus. We are his handiwork. But sometimes the strings break. In this fallen world, Satan will do all that he can to keep us from becoming everything God created us for. We must hold fast to the belief that God is making something special in our lives to put his grace on display before a watching world.

The biblical author James gives us clear application for responding to Satan's attacks:

> *Submit yourselves, then, to God. Resist the devil, and he will flee from you. Come near to God and he will come near to you. Wash your hands, you sinners, and purify your hearts, you double-minded. Grieve, mourn and wail. Change your laughter to mourning and your joy to gloom. Humble yourselves before the Lord, and he will lift you up. (James 4 v 7-10)*

How is Satan trying to lure *you* away from God's design for your life? How might you resist the devil? How can you draw near to God?

Are you willing to humble yourself before God? If not, he has a way, as with my UFO, of humbling us. We can humble ourselves or we can be humbled. We can listen and learn—or we can live and learn.

As you make your way in the wild you can be "confident of this, that he who began a good work in you will carry it on to completion until the day of Christ Jesus" (Philippians 1 v 6). God's Spirit will work in you so you might let your "light shine before others, that they may see your good deeds and glorify your Father in heaven" (Matthew 5 v 16).

This is what it looks like to live the Christian life in the fallen world. It's not going to be easy. But you already knew that, didn't you?

In the wild, in these roles we are assigned during this earthly intermission, God is doing something remarkable in our lives if we will let him. It will be messy, but it will be worth it. He can make a rose bloom even in the midst of thorns. Our faith can flourish in the wild with the help of the One who overcame Satan and the grave.

CHAPTER 7

GOD'S FINAL ENEMY

"And the LORD God commanded the man, 'You are free to eat from any tree in the garden; but you must not eat from the tree of the knowledge of good and evil, for when you eat from it you will certainly die.'"

GENESIS 2 v 16-17

"What else is there to be afraid of?" asks Siggy, a young boy in the movie *What About Bob?* Siggy and Bob, the main character of the film played by Bill Murray, share a morbidly humorous dialogue on the topic of death, in which the child lectures the adult. "There's no way out," the boy says. "You're going to die. I'm going to die. It's going to happen. What difference does it make if it's tomorrow or eighty years? … What else is there to be afraid of?"

Does it make any difference if your death is tomorrow or eighty years from now, as Siggy asked? I bet it matters to you. I imagine you'd prefer to live to see more than just one more day. But the boy is right. Death will come for us all eventually. We spend most of our lives trying to avoid it.

Nothing seems more unnatural to us than death. We all know we will die, yet it seems almost an impossibility to us—nearly inconceivable. No matter how much we think we've come to grips with living in a universe where death is inevitable, it still seems to surprise us. We all think we will get to see another day.

But what if we don't? What if this is the last book you will ever read? I'd better not say that—you might go pick up a better book.

But think about it: the obituaries roll out every morning. We read about death daily in the news. Coffee and dead people: it's the morning tradition. But still it is jarring when someone we know or love dies. Why is it that death shocks us as it does? Shouldn't we be used to it by now?

The Birth of Death

My brother Chris, a photojournalist for the military, volunteers for an organization that helps parents remember their children who die either in birth or shortly thereafter. He told me that it's one of the most difficult things he's ever done. That's not a trivial statement coming from a person who has captured images of war on multiple deployments to the Middle East.

He will often be called in shortly after a child passes away. He brings his equipment into the hospital room with him. Often, not always, the parents are present. During the shoots he will look away, or fidget with equipment, when it becomes difficult for him to keep his emotions at bay in order to keep the attention on the family and this final moment.

This final moment...

In a delivery room that should be the scene of great joy, my brother documents death: cold, heartless, relentless death.

Like these precious babies, we will all face a final moment. Most of us try to distract ourselves from this thought. As Siggy asked, "What else is there to be afraid of?"

God warned Adam about this. He told him that he would die if he disobeyed. I guess Adam wasn't a very good rule-follower. Neither are we.

But Adam didn't die physically right away, did he? Spiritually he died the moment he rebelled against God (Ephesians 2). The death of his body was enacted when he was exiled from Eden and no longer had access to the tree of life (Genesis 3 v 24). He and Eve were created to live, truly live, in God's presence with his provision in the garden.

But now they were exiles, spiritually dead and physically dying. The moment they rebelled against God something inside them choked—oxygen was cut off from their souls. Gasping for air they were banished from God's presence. Their souls now dead because of sin, they were no longer fit to live in the garden.

And now, without the daily nourishment of the tree of life, severed from divine life-support, their bodies would slowly catch up with their souls. In the wild, death would reign, both spiritual and physical. Death has been reigning ever since. It reigns still. But it will not reign forever.

Some Body to Love

What exactly is death? One explanation comes from a philosophy known as *physicalism*. This position presents humans as merely physical beings.

This philosophy says that when we die, we simply cease to exist. We are physical beings and our physical existence is completely dependent upon our physical bodies. We are our bodies. We are the sum of our parts. When our body dies, we are no more.

If you take this perspective to its logical conclusion, then everything we experience as humans can be reduced to physical explanations. The main problem with this view is simply that it's wrong. (How's that for subtlety?)

It's not just wrong on some theoretical level that intellectual snobs might argue about. It's flatly wrong in the face of all of our lived experience. It's proven wrong the moment our feet hit the floor in the morning and our minds are filled with the cares of the day.

The things that mean the most in life cannot be reduced to physical explanations. They just can't. Life is about more than just matter, than physical stuff.

We spend the bulk of our lives living for these things that have no scientific explanation—things that are beyond matter. That's why if you want to understand what it means to be human, you have to give serious thought to all of the non-physical values at the core of the human experience.

For example, consider the human emotion of *love*. Love loses all meaning when reduced to purely physical accounts. We know that there are certain chemical reactions in our brain, and even physiological elements, like hormones, that can be associated with various expressions of love. But is love nothing more than chemical reactions?

Some might suggest that evolutionary instincts—the need to create the next generation—are another major factor in understanding what we call love. But are we really satisfied or convinced with the explanation that a parent's love for their child, or a lover's desire for their partner, is best explained as chemical reactions and survival instincts? Is love nothing more than biological impulses to spread our genes and progress our species?

Or do this—take a two-liter bottle of soda and shake it up. I bet you won't because you know exactly what will happen. There will be a chemical reaction that will result in a carbonated explosion if you untwist the lid. Let me ask you this: is the cola right or wrong? Is the fizz loving or hateful?

If we try to reduce the human experience to exclusively physical categories, we will lose what it means to be human altogether. Since you care for so many things that have no physical explanation—like love, beauty, justice, truth, and so on—why would you ever buy into a view of humanity that only cares about the physical? And if there is a non-physical part of you, then what do you think happens to it when your body dies?

The Bible says our bodies are destined to die and after that we will face judgment (Hebrews 9 v 27). Scripture makes it clear that we will give an account for the life we live in this body (2 Corinthians 5 v 10). That's why Jesus said:

> *Do not be afraid of those who kill the body but cannot kill the soul. Rather, be afraid of the One who can destroy both soul and body in hell. (Matthew 10 v 28)*

We are more than just matter. We are more than just a body. We are body and soul. That's what it means to be human. Only God is able to destroy or save both body and soul. That's why Jesus said we should fear him.

There is something worse than physical death. That means there is a fear that should overshadow our fear of the grave. It is to stand before God under judgment after we die. Like Adam and Eve, without God's forgiveness we will find ourselves naked and ashamed with nowhere to hide.

The idea of judgment after death doesn't make life unimportant. It shows just how important our lives really are. The Bible takes the life of our body and soul very seriously. It shows us that we should be concerned about what will happen the moment after we breathe our last breath.

After all, what else is there to be afraid of?

Our Soul Identity

I've tried to show that it's easy to misunderstand death by only focusing on the physical dimension of the human experience. But we can also get it wrong by going in the other direction. Another error is to only focus on the spiritual aspect of the human experience. A proper understanding of death must account for both the physical and the spiritual.

There's a quote from the famous novelist George MacDonald that illustrates the problem of focusing only on the spiritual: "You don't have a soul. You are a soul. You have a body."

Is this really the case? Are we really souls who happen to occupy a body for some short time? Are our bodies just some sort of soul-suit—a fashionable garment we wear during our time on earth?

Does death free us to be our true selves, our souls finally liberated from the flesh prison they've been locked in throughout our earthly lives? If that's the case, then why does death seem so monstrous, so unnatural, and so inhumane? Shouldn't it be more of an event to be celebrated, and not a harsh end to something real and meaningful?

The reason death seems so unnatural is because of how we are created. God made us as embodied souls. That means we are both our soul and our body. Theologians refer to this as the human *dichotomy*, meaning we are more than just one thing.

Look back at how God designed humanity in Genesis:

> *Then the LORD God formed a man from the dust of the*
> *ground and breathed into his nostrils the breath of life,*
> *and the man became a living being. (Genesis 2 v 7)*

Here we discover that Adam is more than just matter, because God breathed the breath of life into him—what Christians understand as a *soul*. But Adam is also more than just a soul, because God created him out of the dust of the ground. So Adam is both material and immaterial, both body and soul.

This means death is the loss of a significant part of us. It is the loss of a major property of our humanity, of how we are created to be. Our bodies are not an afterthought to God but an important part of our humanity. We are more than our bodies, but we are not less.

This is the tragedy of the grave: our soul is severed from our body. Even Jesus cried at the sight of those mourning the death of his friend Lazarus. Death rips apart our humanity.

When a loved one dies, we know that their soul continues to live. And we know that for the believer to be away from the body is to be at home with the Lord (2 Corinthians 5 v 8). But this doesn't make funerals easy or painless. It doesn't altogether undo grief.

That's why it's not completely accurate when someone at a funeral says, "That's not really so and so. They are with the Lord." Our body is a part of who we are. That really is so and so in the coffin. It's just not all of them. Death has separated their body from their soul. As the Bible says, the dust returns to dust and the spirit returns to God, who gave it (Ecclesiastes 12 v 7).

Our Hope in Death

The sting of death reminds us in a powerful way of the consequences of sin, of the warning given to Adam in the garden before the fall. The ripping apart of soul and body in death is a potent picture of the result of human rebellion. It is indeed something to be grieved.

From the time of the fall in the garden, humans have not been fully oriented toward God in either our body or our soul. But God's salvation is complete, including both soul and body, resulting in the full redemption of the entire person.

Our souls are made right with God when we experience a life-transforming encounter with Jesus in this life. This is what Christians call *conversion*. But beyond this life Christians will receive a new body—one that is free from corruption. This is what Scripture describes as *resurrection*. Believers will then be able to entirely obey what Jesus called the greatest commandment: to love God with all of our heart, soul, mind, and strength (Mark 12 v 30).

That means that death for the believer, though painful and real and tragic, is the beginning of a complete restoration of what it means to be human. As C.S. Lewis wrote in his book *The Problem of Pain*, "To enter heaven is to become more human than you ever succeeded in being on earth."

But we still grieve the physical loss of our brothers and sisters in Christ, as the apostle Paul explains, but we do not grieve as those without hope:

> *Brothers and sisters, we do not want you to be*
> *uninformed about those who sleep in death, so that you*
> *do not grieve like the rest of mankind, who have no*
> *hope. For we believe that Jesus died and rose again, and*
> *so we believe that God will bring with Jesus those who*
> *have fallen asleep in him. (1 Thessalonians 4 v 13-14)*

But what exactly is our hope in death? The Christian's hope is that God will clothe us with a new body that we might, as we were originally designed to, live in his presence. Our hope is that we will worship God as we were created to, fully loving him in body and soul.

That's why Christians must not trivialize death by dealing with it only on a theoretical level, or by dealing with it only as something of spiritual significance. We must inform both our grief and our hope with the promises of God.

This is how Paul is able to refer to physical aging, suffering, persecution, and death as "light and momentary" in comparison to our future state, which he describes as an eternal weight of glory (2 Corinthians 4 v 17). For the Christian, there is something infinitely better on the other side of the grave. This life, Paul tells us, simply cannot compare.

We Shall Be Clothed

Speaking of comparisons, let's contrast what God did for Adam and Eve after they rebelled against him with what God has promised to do for those who trust him for salvation. When Adam and Eve first disobeyed God, they realized they were naked. Their shame was associated with their guilt. The first thing they did was to make garments out of fig leaves to cover their nakedness (Genesis 3 v 7).

This is why you see censored versions of Eden, often in children's Bibles, with Adam and Eve wearing strategically-placed fig leaves while they enjoy the garden. Religious children's books often confuse the biblical storyline in this way—but they are wrong because the first couple didn't make coverings for themselves until after they disobeyed God and experienced shame.

And we quickly learn in Genesis that their efforts to cover themselves were insufficient. God replaced their meager fig-leaf wardrobe with clothing made from animal skins (Genesis 3 v 21). This powerful act pictures how God would cover their shame through sacrifice. But an animal sacrifice was not, and is not, God's final method for covering shame.

These things in the garden—the promise of a serpent-crushing child, the animal sacrifice to cover their nakedness—are pointers. They point to the work of Jesus, who would ultimately provide an eternal covering for human guilt and shame.

Adam and Eve, who once knew only goodness, came to know shame because of their disobedience. This serpent-crushing child would take on the consequences of evil so that they—and we—might know pure goodness once again (2 Corinthians 5 v 21). This promised child will make us fit to live in God's presence again. He will clothe our nakedness and lead us back to the garden.

The picture in the Bible is not that we will spend eternity with a forgiven soul and no body, in a kind of ghost-like existence. Nor will we spend eternity as a soul that is reconciled to God but united to a corruptible body. That would make us like zombies—creepy animated corpses that are dead on the outside but somehow alive on the inside.

Our future state will look more like that of Adam and Eve in the garden before the fall than anything like that of ghosts or zombies. That's why an image of Eden is forever stamped on the rearview mirror of the human heart. This explains why the Christian never really feels at home in this world. Our citizenship is elsewhere.

Our hearts yearn for what was lost in the garden. As the author of Hebrews says, we are seeking another city, a better one (Hebrews 11 v 15-16). But we are also never fully at home in our bodies. We long for both soul and body to be fully restored to God's perfect design. We want to again live in his presence and experience his goodness.

The apostle Paul summarizes this beautifully:

> *But our citizenship is in heaven. And we eagerly await a Savior from there, the Lord Jesus Christ, who, by the power that enables him to bring everything under his control, **will transform our lowly bodies** so that they will be like his glorious body.*
> *(Philippians 3 v 20-21, bold text mine)*

Whether you realize it or not, this is your heart's deepest desire. It's the longing behind every longing, the desire beneath every desire. Nothing else can satisfy it. Nothing else was made to. This is the end for which we were made.

Paul talks about this final restoration, this transformation of our lowly bodies, by using language that connects our past to our future, Eden to Eternity. He describes death as nakedness and shows how God has promised to cover us:

> *For we know that if the earthly tent we live in is destroyed, we have a building from God, an eternal*

> *house in heaven, not built by human hands. Meanwhile*
> *we groan, longing to be clothed instead with our*
> *heavenly dwelling, because when we are clothed, **we***
> ***will not be found naked**. For while we are in this*
> *tent, we groan and are burdened, because we do not*
> *wish to be unclothed but to be clothed instead with*
> *our heavenly dwelling, so that what is mortal may be*
> *swallowed up by life. Now the one who has fashioned us*
> *for this very purpose is God, who has given us the Spirit*
> *as a deposit, guaranteeing what is to come.*
> *(2 Corinthians 5 v 1-5, bold text mine)*

Death brings us face to face with the most powerful of all human experiences, reminding us of the severe consequences of sin. Sadly, we tend to face death in the same way Adam and Eve responded to God in the garden. We try to hide. We try to pass the buck. We try to cover ourselves as best as possible.

But God has something better. He has promised to cover our nakedness through sacrifice. As with Adam and Eve, God will indeed clothe us. And because of the dying and rising of Jesus, God has promised to clothe us with a glorious body that we might be like him and be fit to live in his presence.

Jesus' incarnation, when he took on human flesh, shows us that he humbled himself to become like us. His resurrection shows us that we will become like him. His life leads to a complete reversal of the curse of sin. Like in *The Lion, The Witch and the Wardrobe*, once evil is defeated, death begins to work backwards.

Jesus turns the curse on its head. Adam and Eve's disobedience resulted in their being exiled from God's presence in the garden. They were forced into the wild to face the slow process of their bodies catching up with the death of their souls. Christians experience the opposite.

Those who place their faith in Jesus discover abundant and eternal life for their souls. And in the resurrection, they are given the promise of a body fit for their now-living soul, an incorruptible body that is fit to again live in God's presence. That's why Jesus ascending into heaven—what Christians call the ascension—is such a big deal.

Since Adam and Eve were kicked out of the garden, no human has physically dwelled with God (John 3 v 13). But this dramatically changed forty days after Jesus rose from the dead, when the Father took him back to heaven and seated him on a throne at his right hand to serve as our High Priest and King.

Jesus, physically, bodily, now stands in the presence of God, where he intercedes for us. He is praying for us, praying for you, even now, even as you read these words.

Jesus is our representative: humanity again dwelling with the Father. Jesus is the way, the truth, and the life. He is the only way to the Father (John 14 v 6). Jesus opened the door for us to one day return to the place of perfect peace that was lost in Eden. To accomplish this, God's final enemy, death itself, has to die.

No one knows the day or the hour when this definitive defeat will come. It feels like it cannot come soon enough. But the Bible makes it certain: one day death will be placed in a coffin. In the last act of human history, we will read death's obituary.

What else is there to be afraid of?

CHAPTER 8
THE DIVINE COMEDY

*"[God] will swallow up death forever. The Sovereign
LORD will wipe away the tears from all faces; he
will remove his people's disgrace from all the earth
… In that day they will say, 'Surely this is our God;
we trusted in him … let us rejoice and be glad in
his salvation.' "*

ISAIAH 25 V 8-9

I f we're going to experience redemption, someone else has
to write our story. We've proven that we can't write a very
good one for ourselves. We've learned this lesson the hard way.

C.S. Lewis describes this in his famous work *Mere
Christianity*:

*What Satan put into the heads of our remote ancestors
was the idea that they could "be like gods"—could set
up on their own as if they had created themselves—be
their own masters—invent some sort of happiness for
themselves outside God, apart from God.*

> *And out of that hopeless attempt has come nearly all*
> *that we call human history—money, poverty, ambition,*
> *war, prostitution, classes, empires, slavery—the long*
> *terrible story of man trying to find something other than*
> *God which will make him happy.*

History is indeed the human nightmare of realizing we cannot fabricate true, lasting happiness apart from God's presence and provision. We've been rehearsing this lesson since we left the garden. Experience keeps showing us that we tend to make a mess of things.

Yet we still just want our piece of fruit from the tree of the knowledge of good and evil. We so easily think, "Who needs God? We can decide what is good without him. We can make the most of life in the wild."

These are common lies. Most of us are savvy enough not to speak them out loud, but that doesn't mean we've never thought about them in one way or another. These lies are mile markers along the tear-stained trail leading back to Eden.

That's why the path of history is paved with regret. We've chosen to live and learn instead of listening to and heeding the words of the Creator. We've paid a high price for our moral autonomy.

The effects of our rebellion, of the fall, are daunting. We are exiles living in a dangerous land. Our relationships with the Creator, with each other, and even with the land, are severed or strained. Our moral confusion makes the pathway unclear. Satan seeks to ambush us. Death seals our destiny.

Most days it doesn't seem as if things are going to get any better. It feels as if we're stuck in the wild and the best that a sermon, or a book like this, can do is kind of rub our nose in our misfortune. Maybe we should just resign ourselves to a life of hardship. After all, we deserve it. Why shouldn't we simply lower our expectations and hope to be pleasantly, even if mildly, surprised?

Good Grief

Maybe we can try to get on with life, like Charlie Brown, who starred alongside his loyal pet beagle, Snoopy, in the comic strip *Peanuts*. If you've ever read *Peanuts*, you know you can't help but love Charles, with his yellow shirt zigzagged with a bold black line, his crooked smile, and scraggly hair. But man did that kid ever have bad luck.

His fate took a turn for the better, however, when he moved from print to the silver screen. In 2015, 20th Century Fox gave Charlie Brown a complete makeover. The movie was brilliant. I loved it. So did my kids.

Charles Schulz, the creator of *Peanuts*, died fifteen years before the movie. He was the inspiration for Charlie Brown, and I'm pretty confident he wouldn't have approved of the film. That's because it departs from the central tone and trajectory around which *Peanuts* was created.

As Charles Schulz explained, "All the loves in the strip are unrequited; all the baseball games are lost; all the test scores are D-minuses; the Great Pumpkin never comes; and the football is always pulled away." Even the little red-haired girl, whom Charlie Brown so admired, was based on a real red-haired girl who turned down Charles Schulz's marriage proposal.

In an interview about a year before his death he said, "All of a sudden I thought, 'You know, that poor, poor kid, he never even got to kick the football. What a dirty trick—he never had a chance to kick the football.'" Schulz seemed to carry this sense of frustration and disappointment with him to the grave, dying shortly after being diagnosed with colon cancer, on the eve of the publication of his final comic strip.

But the new *Peanuts* movie accomplished something that the comic strip never could—the redemption of Charlie Brown. In the 2015 film, he finally has his day. His good deeds are recognized. He writes a stellar paper for a school assignment. He successfully flies a kite. And, perhaps most importantly, he wins the affection of the little red-haired girl.

And even though in the final scene he still misses the football, his response tells the whole story. He lands on his back and turns to the camera, eyebrows raised, and reveals a wide, soul-satisfied grin. He found what his author never gave him.

Like with *Peanuts*, we cannot find true soul satisfaction unless we let someone else write our story. Our inner Charlie Brown will only be saved if someone else takes over the plot.

The Hinge of History

If our fingers continue to grip the pen and paper, we'll only get more of the same. God will not rip them away from us. We must lay them down. We must surrender.

The writing instruments we use to pen our narratives are weapons we try to fend God away with. He wants us to freely give him supreme authorship over the story of our lives. He can write a better one.

Only God can turn the human tragedy into a divine comedy.

We will not find authentic, sustainable flourishing by ignoring or breaking God's laws. Just as we cannot ignore God's physical laws, like gravity, without consequence, neither can we break his moral laws without consequence. We need his help. We've violated his laws, and our lives are living proof that lasting happiness is not found outside his presence and provision.

To begin, we have to quit insisting on defining for ourselves what is good. We must return to his words and his ways. We cannot find goodness apart from him. That's why we must stop grasping for the tree of the knowledge of good and evil, recognizing that God alone is the one who determines what is good.

The good news is that if we truly desire to live in his presence with his provision, then God offers us not only a new chapter, but in time, a storyline so glorious and so dramatic that the apostle Paul says it cannot even compare to our past or present suffering and heartache.

> *I consider that our present sufferings are not worth comparing with the glory that will be revealed in us. For the creation waits in eager expectation for the children of God to be revealed. (Romans 8 v 18-19)*

In Christ we are offered a restored relationship with God. And through him we are able to find reconciliation and renewed relationships with each other. As we grow in our relationship with Christ, we may learn to walk in his wisdom, heeding and applying his words to our lives. We'll receive strength to move his moral commands from the peripheral to the center of our vision, knowing they are given for our good and his glory.

This isn't to say that life in the wild will be an easy, steady path. It will not. The Bible portrays the Christian life as marked by struggle, progress, disappointment, mourning, longing, and expectation (Romans 7). But in Christ we discover a hope that overshadows even the grave, knowing that death is not final. There's more to the story.

The grave does not have the final word. There's another act, a divine act that uproots death. Our lives are spent in autumn and winter. Spring is coming.

Creation on Tiptoes

That's why we long for Christ's return, along with the groaning creation, anticipating God's final act in human history when he comes to make all things new (Romans 8 v 22-23). Like the prodigal son, in Christ we find complete acceptance and a celebration, and anticipate a future feast (Luke 15; Revelation 19). Then we will once more live in God's presence and experience his goodness.

The final divine act will bring an end to man's *long terrible story of trying to find something other than God which will make him happy*. Between acts, God is waiting patiently, his kindness intended to lead us to repentance (Romans 2 v 4). While it is still today, in what I have described as our earthly intermission, God calls us to respond to him in faith (Hebrews 3 v 13-15).

God asks us to trust *him* to write our story. He offers us his forgiveness and his friendship. His promise to help us make it in the wild is coupled with the hope that one day he will receive us home.

But God will not wait forever. A day is coming when all things will bow to his sovereign will, and every person will acknowledge him one way or another (Philippians 2 v 10). The apostle Paul describes this final earthly scene:

> *Then the end will come, when he hands over the*
> *kingdom to God the Father after he has destroyed all*
> *dominion, authority and power. For he must reign until*
> *he has put all his enemies under his feet. The last enemy*
> *to be destroyed is death. (1 Corinthians 15 v 24-26)*

Christ's return will fulfill what the prophet Isaiah spoke of: death will be swallowed up in victory (Isaiah 25 v 8; 1 Corinthians 15 v 54-55). We've been waiting for this our entire lives. All of our hopes, all our optimism, are wrapped up in this promise of a serpent-crushing child bringing us back to God's presence and provision. Eden will be restored.

When he comes, our pilgrimage in the wild will finally be over. We will be home. Through Christ, all will be made new, and once again all we'll know will be the goodness and glory of God, living again in his presence with his provision. Here's how the apostle John explains this future reality:

> *Then I saw "a new heaven and a new earth," for the*
> *first heaven and the first earth had passed away, and*
> *there was no longer any sea. I saw the Holy City, the*
> *new Jerusalem, coming down out of heaven from God,*
> *prepared as a bride beautifully dressed for her husband.*
> *And I heard a loud voice from the throne saying, "Look!*
> *God's dwelling-place is now among the people, and he*
> *will dwell with them. They will be his people, and God*
> *himself will be with them and be their God. 'He will*
> *wipe every tear from their eyes. There will be no more*
> *death' or mourning or crying or pain, for the old order*
> *of things has passed away." He who was seated on the*
> *throne said, "I am making everything new!"*
> *(Revelation 21 v 1-5)*

Les Misérables

Sometimes a book, a poem, or a movie will strike a chord within my heart, resonating with this future vision. For me, it's generally when I don't really expect it. As C.S. Lewis describes, we are usually *surprised by joy*.

One powerful example for me is the film of Victor Hugo's novel *Les Misérables*. I'll admit I didn't read the one-thousand-plus-page book. Forgive me. Sometimes it's easier to wait for the movie.

The story is a contrast between grace and law illustrated through the lives of a criminal named Jean Valjean and a determined detective named Javert. Jean Valjean serves a nineteen-year sentence for stealing a loaf of bread and multiple attempted escapes. After he is released on parole, he meets a bishop whose kindness and care leads to his conversion to Christianity.

Valjean, now a changed man, vows to live a new life. He assumes a new identity, and though breaking his parole, finds success as a businessman running a factory, and eventually becomes town mayor. But Javert never tires of seeking to capture Valjean.

Valjean stays true to his word and uses his success to care for the less fortunate, *the miserable ones*, for whom the story is named. In the end, in a complete role-reversal, Valjean is in a position to judge and execute Javert. Valjean, as a man who has received grace, offers grace to the man who ruthlessly pursued him his entire life. But Javert remains true to his character as well. Unable to reconcile grace with law, Javert takes his own life instead.

In the final scene, Jean Valjean is near death. It was at this point that I found myself holding back tears as I watched a Hollywood depiction of a forgiven man entering eternity.

Valjean joins a chorus of "the miserable ones" whose lives, while meager on earth, are transformed into a singing choir welcoming Valjean home.

In the end their misery is turned into something beautiful, suggesting that, perhaps, the truly miserable ones are those, like Javert, who never accepted grace. Strangely enough, they sing of the freedom they have found in the garden of the Lord. The images of these men and women, adults and children, speaking of the rising of the sun, shouting songs of redemption, moved me in a powerful way.

That's because it is a reflection of a real future promised in Scripture.

An Ending That Upends Everything

Images like these move us because we live in a fallen world where it seems we are constantly fighting for faith. We long for this future reality. The reminders of the consequences of our sin surround us in the wild. We hear about it in the news. We see it in the mirror.

That's why we must daily fix our eyes on the only One who can help us. As a friend of mine, David Gunderson, once said on Twitter:

> *Run to Jesus. If you can't run, crawl. If you can't crawl, reach. If you can't reach, look.*

Sometimes the best we can do is merely look, but God is strong enough to use even weak faith. The key is not the strength of our faith but the power of God.

One day a trumpet will sound and God's power will be on full display. At the appointed time, the Father will send the

Son for the closing act of human history. It is in this promise that the apostle Paul says we should find our encouragement:

> *According to the Lord's word, we tell you that we who are still alive, who are left until the coming of the Lord, will certainly not precede those who have fallen asleep. For the Lord himself will come down from heaven, with a loud command, with the voice of the archangel and with the trumpet call of God, and the dead in Christ will rise first. After that, we who are still alive and are left will be caught up together with them in the clouds to meet the Lord in the air. And so we will be with the Lord forever. Therefore encourage one another with these words. (1 Thessalonians 4 v 15-18)*

Now we see this promise dimly. On that day it will be clear that it's not we who are fighting for faith after all. Faith has been fighting for us all along. Like the miserable ones in *Les Misérables*, we will find our joy in the garden of the Lord.

Then we'll realize completely the truth of Psalm 16:

> *You make known to me the path of life; you will fill me with joy in your presence, with eternal pleasures at your right hand. (Psalm 16 v 11)*

His presence is where we were always meant to dwell.

Paradise was lost in Adam. Paradise will be restored through Christ. At his right hand, there are pleasures ever more.

If Christ's return is the closing act of history, then what we see in the book of Revelation, written by the apostle John, is a glimpse of the opening act of eternity, or at least our part in it. This vision looks a lot like Eden, but it's even better.

The New Garden

Unlike Eden, in John's vision there's no need for the sun. The Lamb, Christ himself, will be our light. In the new creation, as in the garden, we will again see God's face. In the light of his countenance we will be surrounded by life:

Then the angel showed me the river of the water of life, as clear as crystal, flowing from the throne of God and of the Lamb down the middle of the great street of the city. On each side of the river stood the tree of life, bearing twelve crops of fruit, yielding its fruit every month. And the leaves of the tree are for the healing of the nations. No longer will there be any curse. The throne of God and of the Lamb will be in the city, and his servants will serve him. They will see his face, and his name will be on their foreheads. There will be no more night. They will not need the light of a lamp or the light of the sun, for the Lord God will give them light. And they will reign for ever and ever. (Revelation 22 v 1-5)

This scene will only take place after the curtain closes on the human struggle. Human history—the terrible story of man's search for happiness apart from God, our quest to define goodness on our own—will come to a sudden end. That's why John's vision of the future is accented with urgency. *"Look, I am coming soon!"* John is told (Revelation 22 v 7).

The earthly intermission will end abruptly. That's why Paul says we must awake from our slumber, because our salvation is nearer than when we first believed (Romans 13 v 11). But until that day, we look to the eastern sky with anticipation for the return of the serpent-crushing child who, once conquering his final enemy, death, will welcome us home like the father of the prodigal son.

Then he is going to throw an amazing party. The Bible refers to it as the wedding supper of the Lamb (Revelation 19 v 9). We will have every good reason to celebrate. We, the miserable ones, the prodigal sons and daughters, will be at home with our Redeemer.

Our suffering will cease. The curse will be no longer. Sin will never again entangle our souls. No child will ever again be abused. Cancer won't take another life. Divorce won't separate another family. The seas of natural disaster will be stilled. The grave will have lost its sting. Addiction will be erased. Evil will be vanquished. Death will have died.

We will be fit to again live in God's presence with his provision. At his right hand, we will experience fullness of joy and pleasures forevermore. We will only know good. And on that day, we too will sing songs of redemption, of life, in the Lord's garden.

On that glorious day, he will welcome us home, *out of the wild.*

AFTERWORD
DEATH'S OBITUARY

Death follows hard after breathing beings
He's not stopping 'til he freeze your feelings,
Or seize your nerves and leave you reeling

This is no joke: you've been told before
It's too late when he's knocking at your door

But the Devil's surprise, can't believe his eyes,
The hinges whine, he discovers his prize

Before him stands an Innocent Lamb
Nailed him down, crucified I Am

Buried him deep, then locked the door
Threw away the keys, but please, there's more
What God had in store,
Sent Death through the floor

High King of Calvary, the prisoners set free,
Though slain, now raised, claiming victory

Yes!

And now we read: Death's Obituary

THANK YOU

It is fitting for me to give thanks first and foremost to Jesus. I had a life-transforming encounter with him when I was fifteen. I've never gotten over it. I'm far from having arrived, but he is faithful to finish what he started. I'm banking on that.

I want to thank my family. April, you encourage me in all of these endeavors in ways you don't even realize. I love being yours. Isaiah, your love for reading makes my love for writing all the more enjoyable. Micah, your creative mind never ceases to amaze me. (I'm sure the *Action Cats* are going to be a bestseller!) Josiah, your little smile lights up my world. Addilynn Joy, you are my joy-bird. You're so sweet, I could eat you up—like some popcorn (you will appreciate this when you are older).

I want to thank The Good Book Company for the opportunity to work on this and other projects. It has been a pleasure. Your British hospitality has caused me to have mixed emotions when celebrating the Fourth of July.

Alison, you are a patient, kind, godly, encouraging editor and friend. Thank you for investing in my writing. The benefits in my life and in the development of my craft will far surpass the printing of this book.

Thank you to the students at Word of Life Bible Institute. I told you guys I would give you a shout out when I was teaching up there for a week in the early fall of 2016. "Drink Coffee, Listen to Gangster Rap, and Deal With It" is the message on the coffee cup one of you gave me. I use it often.

To Nick Scott, for all the help you provided while serving at Boyce College. You were a tremendous blessing from helping with research projects, to organizing events, to heading up our annual Boston trip. Thank you for your servant leadership.

To my students at Cedarville University: it has been a joy getting to know you. It has been wonderful to have you in my classes and in our home. Getting to be around college students is one of the joys of the DeWitt family. You give more to us than we feel we could ever give to you.

To some friends, "I don't know half of you as well as I should like; and I like less than half of you as well as you deserve." Anthony and Matt (F3 for life). Uncle Sam, you're the best Brit on this side of the Atlantic. Billy, Lewis is better than Tolkien. Jeff and Dan (D3 has left the building). To the rest of my L'ville squad, I miss y'all (you know who you are).

COMPANY

BIBLICAL | RELEVANT | ACCESSIBLE

At The Good Book Company, we are dedicated to helping Christians and local churches grow. We believe that God's growth process always starts with hearing clearly what he has said to us through his timeless word—the Bible.

Ever since we opened our doors in 1991, we have been striving to produce resources that honor God in the way the Bible is used. We have grown to become an international provider of user-friendly resources to the Christian community, with believers of all backgrounds and denominations using our Bible studies, books, evangelistic resources, DVD-based courses, and training events.

We want to equip ordinary Christians to live for Christ day by day, and churches to grow in their knowledge of God, their love for one another, and the effectiveness of their outreach.

Call us for a discussion of your needs or visit one of our local websites for more information on the resources and services we provide.

Your friends at The Good Book Company

NORTH AMERICA
UK & EUROPE
AUSTRALIA
NEW ZEALAND

thegoodbook.com
thegoodbook.co.uk
thegoodbook.com.au
thegoodbook.co.nz

866 244 2165
0333 123 0880
(02) 9564 3555
(+64) 3 343 2463

WWW.CHRISTIANITYEXPLORED.ORG
Our partner site is a great place for those exploring the Christian faith, with a clear explanation of the good news, powerful testimonies and answers to difficult questions.